Enjoy!
You will use more
than me!

AP.

SIMPLY

Inspirational & Delicious

RAW DESSERTS TO ENJOY!

KELLY PARR

SWEET ENCOUNTER

ISBN: 9780982837979

Printed in the United States of America.

Purpose Publishing
1503 Main Street, #168
Grandview, MO 64030

Book Design & Layout by: Sharon Dailey
Design © 2012 Sharon Dailey Design

Disclaimer: The materials in this document or any of the materials associated with Freedom Quest International are for educational purposes only and are not meant to diagnose, prescribe, cure or prevent an illness in any way. We are not attempting to replace professional medical care. We believe it is valuable to seek the advice of a qualified alternative health care professional before making any life changes.

For more information please contact:

Freedom Quest International
PO Box 8631
Kansas City, MO. 64114-0631

Email: kelly@freedomquestinternational.org
blog: www.kellyparr.org
web: www.freedomquestinternational.org

TABLE OF CONTENTS

ABOUT

THE AUTHOR

Kelly Parr

Kelly is an international teacher with a passion to see lives restored, refreshed and released into a greater level of wholeness – body, soul and spirit. As a Bible teacher, Doctor of Naturopathy and Natural Health Counselor, Kelly graduated in Feb 2001 from the College of Natural Health, founded by Dr. Joel Robbins. Whether from her kitchen or the pulpit, Kelly imparts freedom to the whole person as she communicates with honesty, transparency and humility.

Kelly and her husband Bob have traveled to over 18 countries and lived in SE Asia as missionaries for 15 years. They are the co-founders of *Freedom Quest International*, a 501(c)(3) non-profit ministry that brings a unique and life transforming message world-wide. They teach on subjects such as the Father's Heart, Sonship, Marriage & Family, Fasting, and Health & Nutrition. Together, Bob and Kelly are the parents of five children and reside in the Kansas City, Missouri area.

THE PHOTOGRAPHER

Johnna Brynn

Kelly's daughter Johnna is an international photographer who has traveled to over 20 countries and currently resides near the beautiful bay of Sarasota, Florida. She is the founder of *Star Shooter: phototherapy for kids*, a 501(c)(3) non-profit organization, since July 2008, and started Johnna Brynn Photography, LLC in March 2009.

Johnna has a masters degree in psychology and is currently pursuing a PhD in psychology.

Johnna is known for her keen eye and ability to capture emotions in those fleeting moments that create timeless memories. Her creative sensibilities and international experience allow her to capture subjects on camera with a discerning, yet refreshing perspective.

FRESH

BODY

SOUL

"Sweet Encounter with Raw Desserts" is more than just recipes. It's a mother and daughter coming together, creating a raw dessert book that will give you a fresh start in every area of your life: body, soul and spirit.

Within these pages, you will discover...

- more than 90 tantalizing guilt-free raw desserts,
- 3 generations of prize winning dessert recipes (not raw!)
- over 50 motivating tips that will encourage and educate
- how Kelly stocks her pantry and a list of her favorite kitchen gadgets
- Johnna's creative, inspiring and mouth-watering photography

Any type of life change begins with small steps, so what better way to transition into a fresh start than with healthy raw desserts. Besides, smoothies are a great way to sneak in some greens (shhh…don't tell my son Josh)!

For a fresh start, try these recipes and have your own "Sweet Encounter" body, soul and spirit!

From our kitchen to yours,

Kelly & Johnna

GIVING THANKS

This recipe book would not be what it is without giving thanks to the three generations of fabulous cooks who have gone before me. I am who I am today because of the rich deposits these women made into my life.

Great Mom Chamberlain had her cookie jar in the corner of the ole farm house kitchen, always full of her blue ribbon sugar cookies (page 101). She was the one who fasted and interceded on behalf of the generations that followed. I'm proud to say I'm one.

Granny Cripe was the greatest granny ever! As an Art and Home Economics teacher she filled my childhood days with crafts, sewing, cooking and always creating something out of nothing. Granny was the one who was always adding candy red hots and little silver decorative balls to her dessert recipes – she loved pizzazz!

Momma Connie carries the torch proudly from both women, fasting and praying relentlessly for her children, grandchildren and those to come. Mom has taken the family recipes to the next level, making the best cobblers and crisps this side of heaven!

I also want to acknowledge my Dad, who, while growing up, was the one that, without fail, would eat whatever came out of my easy bake oven. He also helped me with the final title of this book! To my husband Bob, who has believed in me and never turns down the title of being my "taste tester"! To my children: Josh, who challenges me and is constantly saying "Mom, you can do it", Johnna, whose amazing photography brings each recipe to life, and Sherry & Chris, who gave me a quiet corner in their homes to finish this book!

JUICES & SMOOTHIES

JUICES

orange burst

hot carrot

grapple green

blood orange

go green

confetti fiesta

liquid greens

green silk

MATCHA GREEN TEA

summertime heat

pink lady

post-workout elixir

SMOOTHIES

almond milk

brazilian date

strawberry vanilla

cantaloupe on ice

papaya splashed with lime

minty melon

5 REASONS TO CHOOSE BLENDTEC®

blue mesquite

tropical bliss

toasted coconut

CRACKIN' COCONUTS

goji berry swirl

blueberry chew

cherry mash

banana berry blizzard

milk-e-way

For the following recipes: wash, chop, dice and peel the fresh fruit and vegetables accordingly. If they are organic there is no need to peel (except for the citrus fruit and kiwi's that is)!

Depending on what type of juicer & blender you have, will determine how small you are able to slice your fruits & veggies, and their size, will determine the amount they yield! Most of the following recipes yield 1-3 servings.

Note: The carob, barley malt, oats, toasted coconut, tofu and maple syrup (grade B) in the following recipes are not considered raw, but are great alternatives for those who are just beginning a raw food adventure!

JUICES

TIP

The Juice of the calamansi lemons will make you pucker! They are native to SE Asia, (particularly the Philippines) and can be found at your local Asian Markets!

ORANGE BURST

Just mentioning the name "starburst" candies makes my mouth water... so I've created a healthier juiced version!

5 carrots
3 oranges

1 green apple
1-2 calamansi lemon

Juice all ingredients in a juicer. The green apple and calamansi lemon give it that tart, bold, make-your-mouth-water experience!

HOT CARROT

Johnna's favorite juice is carrot and orange, mine is carrot and beet. As for Bob, this one is his, especially when I throw in a pinch of 90,000 heat units of cayenne pepper!

8 carrots　　　　　　　　　　　**pinch of cayenne pepper**
2 garlic cloves

Juice carrots and garlic in a juicer diluting with pure water if necessary, then add the pinch of heat!

GRAPPLE GREEN

This simple elixir will jumpstart your metabolism, fight off the common cold, burn fat and flush out excess water weight. So drink up!

2 grapefruits, peeled　　　　　　**1 lemon, peeled**
3 green apples　　　　　　　　　**2 leaves of romaine lettuce**

Juice all ingredients in a juicer. Enjoy!

TIP

The meyer lemon has a smooth mild taste (much different from the calamansi lemon) and is said to be a cross between either a lemon and tangerine or a lemon and mandarin orange. Try for yourself and see what you think!

BLOOD ORANGE

When I first was introduced to a "blood orange" I was amazed! After slicing my first one and seeing the deep, almost blood color, I quickly understood the name.

3 blood oranges　　　　　　　　**1 small beet**
2 red apples　　　　　　　　　　**1 meyer lemon**

Juice all ingredients in a juicer, diluting with pure water if necessary.

GO GREEN

Some say kale is the King of Greens; others say parsley. So I add both!

2 cups fresh pineapple
2 oranges, peeled
1 grapefruit, peeled
1 celery stalk

handful of kale
handful of parsley
½ cup frozen bananas

Juice the pineapple, oranges, grapefruit and celery in a juicer. Pour into a high-powered blender; add the kale, parsley and frozen bananas blending 30-45 seconds. Garnish with parsley, a chunk of pineapple and go green!

CONFETTI FIESTA

Believe it or not, this fun filled drink bursting with flavor was made by accident! I was whipping it up for Johnna to photograph, when the blender cycle finished earlier than I planned leaving all these little specks of color! Boy am I glad it did!

1-2 tomatoes, chopped
½ lemon, peeled
½ lime, peeled
½ inch piece of ginger
1 tablespoon sweet onion, diced

handful of dandelion greens
handful of parsley
1 jalapeño pepper
5 cherry tomatoes
pinch of cayenne pepper

Juice the tomatoes, lemon, lime and ginger in a juicer. Pour into a high-powered blender; add the onion and blend 10–20 seconds. Then, add dandelion greens and parsley, blending a bit more. Last, add the jalapeño and cherry tomatoes, pulsing for a few seconds until you create red and green specs looking like confetti! Pour into glasses, sprinkle with cayenne and parTAY!

A photo is featured on page 5.

TIP

I tend to have a heavy hand when it comes to blending; thinking just one more turn of the blade will do it. Amazing what transpires when we don't overwork something. (Hmmm perhaps that is a good lesson for me and my mouth as well)!

LIQUID GREENS

Overflowing with vitamin A, iron, calcium, potassium, B vitamins and lots of minerals, this array of liquid is a perfect way to take in your portion of daily greens!

3-4 apples
½ lemon, peeled
½ inch piece of ginger root
handful of spinach leaves

handful of dandelion greens
handful of kale
1 teaspoon of chlorella

Juice all ingredients (except chlorella) in a juicer diluting with water if necessary. Pour mixture into a mason jar, add the chlorella powder, tighten the lid and shake well. Pour into a tall slender glass topped with a parsley sprig and serve!

GREEN SILK

Matcha tea adds more green to this beauty and the frozen banana adds the silky cream texture!

1-2 cucumbers
1-2 green apples
a few sprigs of parsley
1 meyer lemon
½-1 cup frozen bananas

1-2 tablespoons of brown rice protein powder

pinch of matcha green tea for more color!

Juice the cucumbers, apples, parsley and lemon in a juicer. Pour mixture and remaining ingredients into a high-speed blender, adding more or less bananas for desired silkiness!

TIP

Try adding a teaspoon of chlorella to your water bottle and drink before, during and after your workout! Chlorella is green algae with high concentrations of chlorophyll, providing high levels of beta carotene, B-12, iron and protein.

TIP

Brown rice protein powder is a great way for vegetarians to add protein to their diet in place of whey protein powders and is also gluten free!

MATCHA

GREEN TEA

Matcha, an antioxidant powerhouse, is a very high quality, finely ground, green tea and is not to be mistaken as a green tea powder. In terms of its nutritional value and antioxidant content, one glass of matcha tea is the equivalent of 10 glasses of green tea!

- A Japanese tea ceremony centers on the preparation, serving, and drinking of this tea

- Used to flavor and dye foods such as soba noodles, green tea ice cream, mochi and a variety of Japanese confectionery

- Burns calories and boosts metabolism

- Does not raise insulin levels

- Great detoxifier & rich in fiber

- Enhances mood, aids in concentration

- Provides vitamin C, selenium, chromium, zinc and magnesium

- Lowers blood sugar and cholesterol

SUMMERTIME HEAT

If outside is not hot enough for you, then the ginger and cayenne pepper in this drink will heat you up real quick! Cayenne pepper is heart healthy, while ginger does a tummy good!

1 cucumber, chopped	1 kiwi, peeled
1 lemon, peeled	handful of dandelion greens
3 celery stalks	pinch of chipotle or
1 pear, chopped	pinch of cayenne pepper
½-1 inch piece of ginger root	

Juice the cucumber, lemon, celery, pear and ginger in a juicer. Pour into a high-powered blender; add the kiwi, dandelion greens and your choice of pepper, blending 30-45 seconds. Relax-n-enjoy!
A photo of this recipe is on page 12.

PINK LADY

Just the name puts a smile on my face and gets my tummy ready to celebrate!

1-2 cucumbers	½ cup frozen red raspberries
1 Meyer lemon, peeled	½ cup frozen bananas
½ cup frozen strawberries	1 tablespoon Aloe vera juice

Juice the cucumbers and lemon in a juicer. Pour mixture into a high-speed blender and add remaining ingredients. Blend for 30-45 seconds, adding pure water as needed.

POST-WORKOUT ELIXIR

After an intense workout you are bound to lose electrolytes, sodium and potassium through sweating. Here is an elixir that will aid in replacing all three!

3 apples	½ cup bananas, frozen
2 celery sticks	

Juice the apple and celery in a juicer. Pour into a high-powered blender; add the frozen bananas to desired thickness.

TIP

For starters, begin with a pinch of the 35,000 HU (heat units) of cayenne and gradually turn it up with a bigger pinch!

TIP

From treating burns, promoting healthy skin, helps digestion, good source of vitamins, increases metabolism, fights against sickness… Aloe vera juice is the one!

SMOOTHIES

ALMOND MILK

Almond milk was my very first introduction to the raw food world! Since then, I have experimented with mixing-n-matching nuts & seeds of all kinds; macadamia, hemp, walnut, cashew, sesame and more. All are chock-full of nutrients, vitamins and easy to digest when presoaked!

1½ cups raw almonds – soaked overnight

2 cups pure water
1 teaspoon sweetener

After soaking, blend almonds in a high-powered blender on high for 20-30 seconds. Add pure water and sweetener to desired taste. The milk then may be strained through a nut milk bag and stored in a refrigerator for up to 2 days.

If you find it difficult to pop the almonds out of their skins after soaking, then blanch them a few minutes and pop em! Almond milk is so versatile that you can use it in any recipes that require milk. Confession…when I'm in a hurry and haven't had time to soak-n-pop almonds, I just grab a handful, throw them in the blender and blend away!

Note: Use pure water when soaking any type of nuts for all nut milk recipes.

TIP

Soaking nuts overnight helps remove the enzyme inhibitors and will aid in digestion and nutrient absorption.

BRAZILIAN DATE

Never stepped on Brazilian soil before, but if I close my eyes while sipping this exotic milk, I come pretty close!

1½ cups raw brazil nuts – soaked overnight

2 cups pure water

1 teaspoon medjool honey date paste (page 78)

½ vanilla bean, scraped

Blend all ingredients in a high-powered blender for 30-45 seconds adding pure water to desired consistency.

Optional: 1 teaspoon alcohol free vanilla may be used in place of vanilla bean.

TIP

Making date paste is so easy! Just take some big plump medjool dates, pit and blend in a food processor with enough water creating a smooth consistency!

STRAWBERRY VANILLA

Who doesn't like strawberries and fresh vanilla beans? Marrying the two, works perfectly poured over a bowl of fresh fruit or used as a base for a smoothie.

½ cup almonds

½ cup fresh strawberries

2 cups pure water

1 teaspoon agave nectar

½ vanilla bean, scraped

Blend all ingredients in a high-powered blender for 30-45 seconds adding pure water to desired consistency.

Optional: 1 teaspoon alcohol free vanilla may be used in place of vanilla bean.

CANTALOUPE ON ICE

This is so simple, elegant and such a crowd pleaser and I'm all about that!

½ cantaloupe   1½ cup pure water

Peel, de-seed and cube the cantaloupe. Blend the cantaloupe cubes in a high-powered blender for 30-45 seconds, adding enough water to desired consistency. Pour into a tall glass over fun shaped ice cubes and serve!

PAPAYA SPLASHED WITH LIME

While living in SE Asia, one of our favorite breakfasts was fresh sliced papaya drizzled with lime juice. It still is. But now when I'm on the go, I just blend it all!

½ papaya   1½ cup pure water
2-4 key limes

Peel, de-seed and cube the papaya. Blend in a high-powered blender for 30-45 seconds adding pure water to desired consistency. Splash on the lime juice to taste.

MINTY MELON

Honeydew is considered the sweetest of all the melons and when blended with just a slight hint of mint, it will produce a cooling sensation in every sip. I especially love the color!

½ honeydew   ½ cup frozen bananas
1-2 mint leaves   1½ cup pure water

Peel, de-seed and cube the honeydew. Blend all ingredients in a high-powered blender for 30-45 seconds adding pure water to desired consistency. Voilà! You not only have a refreshing drink, but one beaming with vitamin C and B6!

TIP

The black seeds of the papaya are edible, but beware as they have a pungent, spicy taste. Dehydrated and then ground they make a great black pepper substitute!

5 REASONS TO CHOOSE

⊚Blendtec®

- Powerhouse – 1560 watts, 3 peak HP & 7 year warranty plus lifetime on the blade!

- Light weight – only 7 lbs! It was so light that I was able to place it in my carry on when flying to Asia.

- Easy to clean- with its wide square bottom, no buttons, flips or knobs, enables this mega machine to be cleaned in a jiffy.

- A no grit machine…. Grinds, blends, liquefies, gets down to business and is used worldwide. With the fancy smart-touch screen, it takes only one touch to start a cycle and automatically shuts off when the cycle is complete. Perfection every time with a taste and texture that can't be beat.

- Pretty – yes this is one of my top five! I love the look especially the sleek smart touch screen fitting perfectly under my cabinet and worth every shiny penny!

As you can see, Blendtec® is the blender of my choice. I use it every day to make smoothies, juice, sauces, salad dressings and more!

TIP

Mesquite powder is sweet like molasses with a slight undertone of caramel. Try adding it to a truffle recipe or sprinkle some over "simply vanilla" ice cream on page 83!

BLUE MESQUITE

Mesquite powder is an excellent source of fiber, is high in protein, and is rich in lysine. Additionally strong in calcium, magnesium, potassium, iron, and zinc, it has a low glycemic level and improves digestion! How's that for a superfood!

2 cups almond milk (page 14)　　**1 cup frozen bananas**
1 cup frozen blueberries　　**1 teaspoon mesquite powder**

Blend all ingredients in a high-powered blender for 30-45 seconds to desired thickness. Pour into fancy glass and top with fresh blueberries!

TROPICAL BLISS

The Hawaiian Islands have the most breathtaking sunsets, incredible sky-high mud pies and delicious coconuts fresh from the tree! It took me awhile to learn how to open a young coconut myself, but once I did there was no turning back!

2 cups almond milk (page 14)
1 cup young coconut meat
1 tablespoon coconut oil
1 tablespoon raw coconut nectar

1 cup frozen pineapple
1 cup frozen raspberries
1-2 cups frozen bananas

Blend all ingredients in a high-powered blender for 30-45 seconds to desired thickness. Pour into a young coconut shell and decorate with edible flowers! Learn to crack your own coconut (page 21).

TOASTED COCONUT

Sunday dinners always included one of Granny's home-made pies. Toasted coconut cream was Gramps' favorite! I know… toasted is not raw, but tradition is important; so here's to Granny!

1 cup almond milk (page 14)
1 cup young coconut meat
1 teaspoon coconut butter
1 teaspoon coconut nectar
2-4 drops stevia, vanilla crème

1 cup frozen bananas
1 tablespoon toasted coconut, shredded
1 tablespoon chopped macadamias

Blend almond milk, coconut meat, coconut butter, coconut nectar and stevia in a high-powered blender. Add frozen bananas and blend to desired thickness. Garnish with toasted coconut and chopped macadamias. Granny would love it!

TIP

If you have any smoothie left over (which I doubt) try pouring it in popsicle molds or ice cube trays and freeze!

COCONUTS

CRACKIN' COCONUTS

This is so easy I can't believe I have waited so long to try it. The more I do it the more confident I feel! All you need is a rubber mallet, old butcher knife, towel and a good steady hand!

Lay a towel on the counter top with plenty of elbow room for choppin'! Set the young coconut on the towel so it doesn't scratch the counter. Next, take a butcher knife in one hand and poke the tip into the top of the coconut, while taking the rubber mallet in the other hand and firmly tapping the knife into the coconut until you feel it go all the way through. Repeat that a few more times, making a square on top of the coconut. Pull back the top, grab a straw and sip away – it's that easy!

BENEFITS OF COCONUT WATER

- **Great blood purifier.**

- **Highest source of electrolytes, making it a superb post-workout drink.**

- **Identical to human blood plasma, making it a great donor.**

- **Used for plasma transfusions to the wounded soldiers during the Pacific War in 1941-45.**

TIP

Finished sipping? Take a spoon and scrape out the meat. Use it to make a smoothie, pudding or freeze it for later use. Amazing huh?!

GOJI BERRY SWIRL

When my husband and I can't decide which fruit smoothie we are hungry for – we have them both!

STRAWBERRY SMOOTHIE

2 cups almond milk (page 14)   **1-2 cups frozen bananas**
1 cup frozen strawberries

BLUEBERRY SMOOTHIE

2 cups almond milk (page 14)   **1-2 cups frozen bananas**
1 cup frozen blueberries

First, make your strawberry smoothie by blending the ingredients in a high-powered blender for 30-45 seconds. Pour into a separate bowl and place in freezer. Next, make the blueberry smoothie in the same way. Remove the strawberry smoothie from the freezer (work quickly!) and use a large spoon to alternate and swirl the smoothie mixtures into fancy glasses. Top with goji berries and you are ready to serve!

TIP

Goji berries are native to China, are rich in Vitamin A, full of powerful anti-oxidants that are said to boost the immune system and lower cholesterol and make a great topping for any smoothie!

BLUEBERRY CHEW

Sometimes I just want something chewy. This seems to do the trick.

2 cups almond milk (page 14)
1 cup frozen blueberries
1-2 cups frozen bananas

1 tablespoon bee pollen
handful of raisins
2-3 dried apricots, chopped

Blend almond milk, frozen blueberries, bananas and bee pollen in a high-powered blender for 30-45 seconds. By adding the bananas in last you can make it as thick as you like. For the chewy part… throw in the raisins, chopped apricots and stir!

CHERRY MASH

One of my fondest memories as a little girl was waking up early in the morning and running to the kitchen to open Gramp's lunch box. Inside I would always discover a special treat – usually a cherry mash!

2 cups almond milk (page 14)
1 cup frozen cherries, pitted

1-2 cups frozen bananas
handful of sweet cacao nibs

Blend almond milk, frozen cherries and bananas in a high-powered blender for 30-45 seconds to desired thickness. Pour into glass and pile on the cacao nibs.

Optional: Using carob chips is yummy too!

BANANA BERRY BLIZZARD

Believe it or not… even in the winter months we still drink our smoothies!

½ cup almonds
¼ cup hemp seeds
1 cup pure water

1 cup frozen mixed berries
1-2 cups frozen bananas
1 teaspoon lucuma powder
(optional)

Blend the almonds and hemp seeds in a high-powered blender until powdered. Add water as needed to make creamy milk. Next add the frozen mixed berries and bananas blending to desired thickness. Finally, blend in the lucuma powder. Enjoy!

TIP

Lucuma has a nutty maple flavor, low glycemic and is a great alternative to any liquid sweetener!

MILK-E-WAY

Swimming on a hot summer day and eating frozen Milky Way bars… those were the days!

2 cups almond milk
1-3 medjool dates, pitted
2 tablespoons organic pure maple syrup (grade B)

1–2 tablespoon raw tahini
(sesame seed butter)
½ vanilla bean, scraped
1-2 cups frozen bananas
handful of carob chips

Blend milk, dates, maple syrup, tahini and vanilla bean in a high-powered blender adding the frozen bananas to desired thickness (I like mine super thick). Pour into a glass, stir in the carob chips and devour!

Optional: 1 teaspoon alcohol free vanilla flavor may be used in place of vanilla bean.

TRUFFLES & BARS

TRUFFLES & BARS

spiced fig truffles

power malt bars

coconut cherry bomb

cashew cup

RAW HONEY

nutty ginger bites

chewy fudge sticks

sin-no-more buns

pink coconut cranberry truffles

HEALTHY SUBSTITUTES

no-bake oat bars

tootsie roll-ups

apple cake truffles

blueberry snowballs

THE FIG & THE DATE

german chocolate truffles

SPICED FIG TRUFFLES

I love to teach about the greatest love song ever- Song of Solomon! There are eight tiny chapters overflowing with delectable goodies, just waiting to be discovered!

Song of Solomon 2:13

"the fig tree has ripened its figs, and the vines in blossom have given forth their fragrance. Arise, my darling, my beautiful one, and come along!"

6-10 figs, chopped
1 cup raw walnuts
1 cup raw almonds

½ cup flax seed
1-2 teaspoon cinnamon
1-2 teaspoon cardamom

COATING

almond flour

Blend the nuts and seeds in a food processor until mixture is crumbly. Add spices to taste. Add figs a little at a time until you can form into small balls. Then roll the balls into very finely ground almonds (almond flour).

POWER MALT BARS

Believe it or not, Johnna does come out from behind her camera and steps into the kitchen—only to create more!

TIP

Barley malt is a whole grain sweetener that is about half as sweet as refined sugar and has a flavor and consistency of molasses.

½ cup raw tahini (sesame seed butter)

½ cup barley malt

¼ cup organic pure maple syrup (grade B)

1 cup oats

3 tablespoons of dried apricots pieces, unsulphured

2 tablespoons sesame seeds

2 tablespoons sunflower seeds

2 tablespoons flax seeds

2 tablespoons pumpkin seeds

2 tablespoons hemp seeds

2 tablespoons pistachio nuts, chopped

Blend together the tahini, barley malt and maple syrup in a food processor. Add enough oats to make a "gooey" dough consistency. Transfer dough to bowl. Blend in the apricots, sesame seeds, sunflower seeds, flax seeds, pumpkin seeds, hemp seeds and pistachio nuts. Lightly grease a square pan with coconut oil and press in the dough. Chill and cut into bars. Thanks Johnna!

Optional: fold in carob chips, raisins or shredded coconut!

COCONUT CHERRY BOMB

This recipe calls for a dehydrator but well worth the experience!

TIP

No dehydrator?

Set your oven on the lowest temperature while keeping the door cracked open during the baking time.

(Check on your goodies every so often as each oven heats differently!)

½ cup almond flour
3½ cups shredded coconut, dried & unsweetened
½ - ¾ cup carob powder

1-1½ cup maple syrup
1 teaspoon vanilla extract
¼ cup coconut oil
cherries, pitted

To make almond flour, blend almonds in a food processor until finely ground. Pour into a large bowl, add shredded coconut and blend. Add carob powder, maple syrup (not raw), vanilla, coconut oil and mix well until it holds its shape when pressed together. Press mixture into a "brownie pop silicone mold" and press a cherry down into the middle making sure the cherry is completely covered with coconut mixture. Chill in refrigerator. Pop out of the mold and dehydrate on 115° for a few hours until crunchy on outside and gooey on inside!

CASHEW CUP

This is a really close taste to raw cookie dough! Another one of Johnna's creations!

1 cup raw cashews
1 cup shredded coconut, dried & unsweetened
⅛ cup raw honey

1 teaspoon vanilla extract
½ cup almond milk
sweet cacao nibs for topping

Blend cashews in a food processor until a fine powder. Add shredded coconut and pulse a few times until mixed. Drizzle and blend in honey, vanilla and enough almond milk to create a "cookie dough" consistency. Using a mini cookie scoop, form into balls and place in mini cupcake liners. Sprinkle with sweet cacao nibs and serve chilled.

Optional: carob chips may be used in place of the sweet cacao nibs.

RAW HONEY

DID YOU KNOW?

The pollen in honey contains all 22 amino acids, 28 minerals, 11 enzymes, 14 fatty acids and 11 carbohydrates.

The ancient Egyptians and Greeks used honey to embalm their dead.

Honey heated at 150° and higher loses its nutritional value.

One spoon of fresh honey, mixed with the juice of half a lemon and warm water makes an effective remedy for constipation and hyperacidity.

Honey is easily digested and assimilated.

Egyptians, Greeks and Romans all discovered that honey rubbed in wounds was a rapid and effective healer.

Honey has the power to make us feel better by improving our mood and to think better by stimulating the part of our brain responsible for learning.

Tradition says that when King David made his triumphant entry into Jerusalem with the Ark, the treats he brought with him were honey cakes.

NUTTY GINGER BITES

These are everyone's favorite no matter what part of the world I'm in!

1 cup raw pecans
1 cup raw almonds
¼ cup flax seeds
1 teaspoon cinnamon
1 teaspoon ginger

½ teaspoon cloves
1½ cup medjool dates, pitted & chopped
1-2 teaspoons of agave nectar

COATING

1 cup almonds, finely ground
½ teaspoon cinnamon powder

¼ teaspoon ginger powder

Blend pecans, almonds, flax seeds and spices in a food processor until chunky. Adjust spices to taste. Add in chopped dates and sweetener, mixing well until the mixture holds its shape when pressed together. Use a mini cookie scoop to form into balls and coat with the mixture of grounded almonds, cinnamon and ginger powder. Chill before serving.

CHEWY FUDGE STICKS

My, my, my, my, my… I can't wait for you to sink your teeth into these chewy delectable raw treats!

1 cup cacao powder

½ cup maple syrup (grade B)

½ cup coconut oil (melted)

1 teaspoon vanilla extract

TOPPINGS

raspberries

hazelnuts, chopped

shredded coconut mixed with cranberry powder

Blend the cacao powder, maple syrup, coconut oil and vanilla in a high powdered blender until creamy. To make the fudge sticks, I used ice-cube molds (the ones shaped for water bottles). First place some chopped fruits, chopped nuts and/or grated fine coconut into each individual mold. Then, spoon in the fudge mixture and press firmly over the topping. Place into freezer to harden. Remove from freezer and pop the chewy fudge sticks out of the molds when ready to devour!

Optional: Carob powder may be used in place of cacao

A photo of this recipe is featured on page 26.

SIN-NO-MORE BUNS

These little delicacies might not keep you from overindulging, but they sure will give you an alternative to satisfying your sweet tooth!

1½ cup raw walnuts

½ cup raw almonds

1 teaspoon cinnamon

1 teaspoon coconut palm sugar

½-1 cup raisins

COATING

raw cane sugar

cinnamon

Blend walnuts and almonds in a food processor until finely chopped. Add cinnamon and sugar and continue to blend. Toss in the raisins and pulse until they are distributed throughout the mixture into small pieces. Form into bite-size balls with your hands and coat with the sugar and cinnamon mixture!

PINK COCONUT CRANBERRY TRUFFLES

These delicate truffles make a sweet Holiday treat… betcha can't eat just one!

1½ cup raw cashews
½ cup raw macadamia nuts
1-1½ cup medjool dates, pitted & chopped
fresh lemon juice to taste

1-2 teaspoons agave nectar
1 tablespoon coconut oil
1 teaspoon vanilla extract
1 cup dried cranberries

COATING

1-2 cups coconut, finely shredded   **1-3 teaspoons cranberry powder**

Blend cashews and macadamia nuts in a food processor into a fine powder. Add dates and blend evenly. Drizzle in fresh lemon juice to taste. Add the agave nectar, coconut oil, vanilla and blend well. Add the dried cranberries and pulse until evenly distributed. Transfer mixture to a bowl and chill in refrigerator for 30 minutes. In the meantime, toss together the coating of shredded coconut and dried cranberry powder.

Form into bite-size balls with your hands. Proceed to coat each ball in the coconut and cranberry mixture. I like to freeze these truffles and take out right before serving. They defrost quickly!

TIP

Got a sweet tooth? Raw almonds dipped in organic honey will satisfy!

HEALTHY
SUBSTITUTES

So many times we just "default" to what we know. But here are a few of my favorite substitutes for the "three biggies"!

WHITE FLOUR

Whole grains such as…
Brown rice
Buckwheat
Ezekiel breads
Kamut

Millet
Quinoa
Soba noodles
Spelt

SUGAR

Agave Nectar
Brown Rice Syrup
Coconut Nectar, raw
Date paste

Honey, raw
Stevia
Sucanat
Yacon syrup

SALT

Bragg's Amino Acids
Kelp granules
Nama Shoyu

Raw Coconut Aminos
Sea Salt

NO-BAKE OAT BARS

These oat bars are a great healthy alternative to store-bought cookies. Not all the ingredients are raw, but you don't have to bake them either!

1 cup almond butter	½ cup oat bran
1 cup brown rice syrup	¼ cup raisins
½ teaspoon almond extract	¼ cup walnut pieces
1 teaspoon vanilla extract	¼ cup carob chips
pinch of sea salt	shredded coconut for topping
2 cups oats (setting 1 cup aside)	

Blend almond butter, brown rice syrup, almond extract, vanilla extract and sea salt in a high powered blender until creamy. In a bowl mix 1 cup oats, bran, raisins, walnuts and carob chips. Pour almond butter mixture over the oat mixture and mix well with a wooden spoon. Add the remaining 1 cup of oats as needed to make a firm dough. If it is not firm enough add more oats. Lightly grease a square pan with coconut oil and press in the dough. Add the shredded coconut on top and press down. Chill and cut into bars. Another one of Johnna's creations!

TIP

Carob is also known as St. John's fruit. Try using carob chips as a substitute for chocolate chips in baking or toss a handful in your favorite trail mix!

TOOTSIE ROLL-UPS

The best recipes are those we discover by accident!

1 cup raw cashews	½ vanilla bean, scraped
2 cups raw walnuts	pinch of sea salt
½ -1 cup cacao powder	
1 teaspoon cinnamon	**CENTER**
¼ cup dark agave nectar	cacao fudge frosting (page 74)

Blend cashews and walnuts in a food processor until a fine powder. Add ½ cup – 1 cup cacao powder depending on your taste. Add cinnamon, dark agave nectar and vanilla bean. Roll out like cookie dough. Spread a layer of cacao fudge frosting over the dough, making sure you spread it all the way to the edges. Roll into a long log. Chill, slice and serve!

Optional: Raw carob powder may be a substitute for the cacao powder.

TIP

English walnuts, also known as the "Royal" nut, are highly prized for the oil they produce. Try drizzling a little over your salad for an extra boost of omega 3 and 6, plus a dose of vitamin E!

APPLE CAKE TRUFFLES

I love digging through old family recipes. Here I added the spices from Granny's "Applesauce Cake" recipe (page 106) and created my own raw version!

1 cup raw almonds

1 cup raw walnuts

1-1½ cup medjool dates, pitted & chopped

1 teaspoon cinnamon

1 teaspoon vanilla extract

⅛ teaspoon of cloves

⅛ teaspoon or less of allspice

½ cup dried apple pieces, unsulphured (rehydrated in fresh apple juice)

COATING

ground almonds

cinnamon

Blend almonds and walnuts in a food processor until a fine powder. Add dates, cinnamon, vanilla, cloves, and allspice blending well. Fold in the rehydrated apple pieces. Form into bite-size balls with your hands and roll in a mixture of ground almonds and cinnamon.

BLUEBERRY SNOWBALLS

Fun to make, fun to eat, whatever time of the year it is!

1½ cup raw cashews

½ cup raw almonds

1-1½ cup medjool dates, pitted & chopped

1 teaspoon cinnamon

½ vanilla bean, scraped

⅛ teaspoon almond extract

coconut nectar to taste

1 cup dried blueberries, unsulphured

COATING

coconut, shredded

Blend cashews and almonds in a food processor until a fine powder. Add dates, cinnamon, vanilla bean, almond extract and coconut nectar blending well. Adjust flavors to your liking. Fold in the dried blueberries. Form into bite-size balls with your hands and roll generously in shredded coconut.

A photo of this recipe is featured on page 36.

TIP

Sulfur dioxide is a chemical used in some dried fruits to keep them "pretty". Be careful, this chemical neither enhances the flavor of the fruit nor the quality and may cause an allergic reaction.

DID YOU KNOW

THE FIG

A fig tree takes three years to bear fruit and grows up to 30 feet or more!

It produces fruit twice a year and can live as long as 400 years!

The fig, a member of the mulberry family, may be baked into cakes and gives you a quick boost of energy.

It has been said that fig "sap" may be an effective element in treating skin cancer.

Oh and we can't forget, it was the fig leaf that clothed Adam and Eve for the first time!

THE DATE

The date is called the bread of the Sahara... where the rich people removed the seed from the date and filled the cavity with butter!

Dates are high in natural aspirin.

Dried fruits (without sulfur dioxide) are linked to lower rates of certain cancers, especially pancreatic cancer.

Soaked dates made into fine syrup make for a great drink with a laxative effect.

Date honey is produced by boiling the dates in water, straining them through a sieve, and continuing to cook the liquid on low heat until thick.

In the Jewish and Christian tradition, the date palm symbolizes life and in poetry it's a symbol of upright stature, justice and righteousness.

GERMAN CHOCOLATE TRUFFLES

I have been inspired by a Texas homemaker!

1 cup raw pecans
½ cup medjool dates, pitted & chopped
¼ cup almond butter
¼ cup dark agave nectar
½ vanilla bean, scraped
1 cup cacao powder
 pinch of sea salt

½ - 1 cup shredded coconut, dried & unsweetened

CENTER
chewy fudge sticks (page 35)

COATING
walnuts, finely chopped
coconut, shredded

First make a batch of the chewy fudge stick dough and roll into small pea size balls. Allow to chill in the refrigerator while making the German chocolate truffle dough.

For the truffle dough: Pulse pecans and chopped dates in a food processor until both nuts and dates are evenly distributed. Add the almond butter, agave, vanilla, cacao powder and salt, blending well. Slowly add enough of the shredded coconut until the mixture holds its shape when pressed together.

Assemble: Using a mini cookie scoop , form a bigger ball of the truffle dough around the small ball of the fudge dough. Roll into the mixture of finely chopped walnuts and coconut. Voilà! You now have my bite size version of German Chocolate Cake!

CAKES, PIES & TARTS

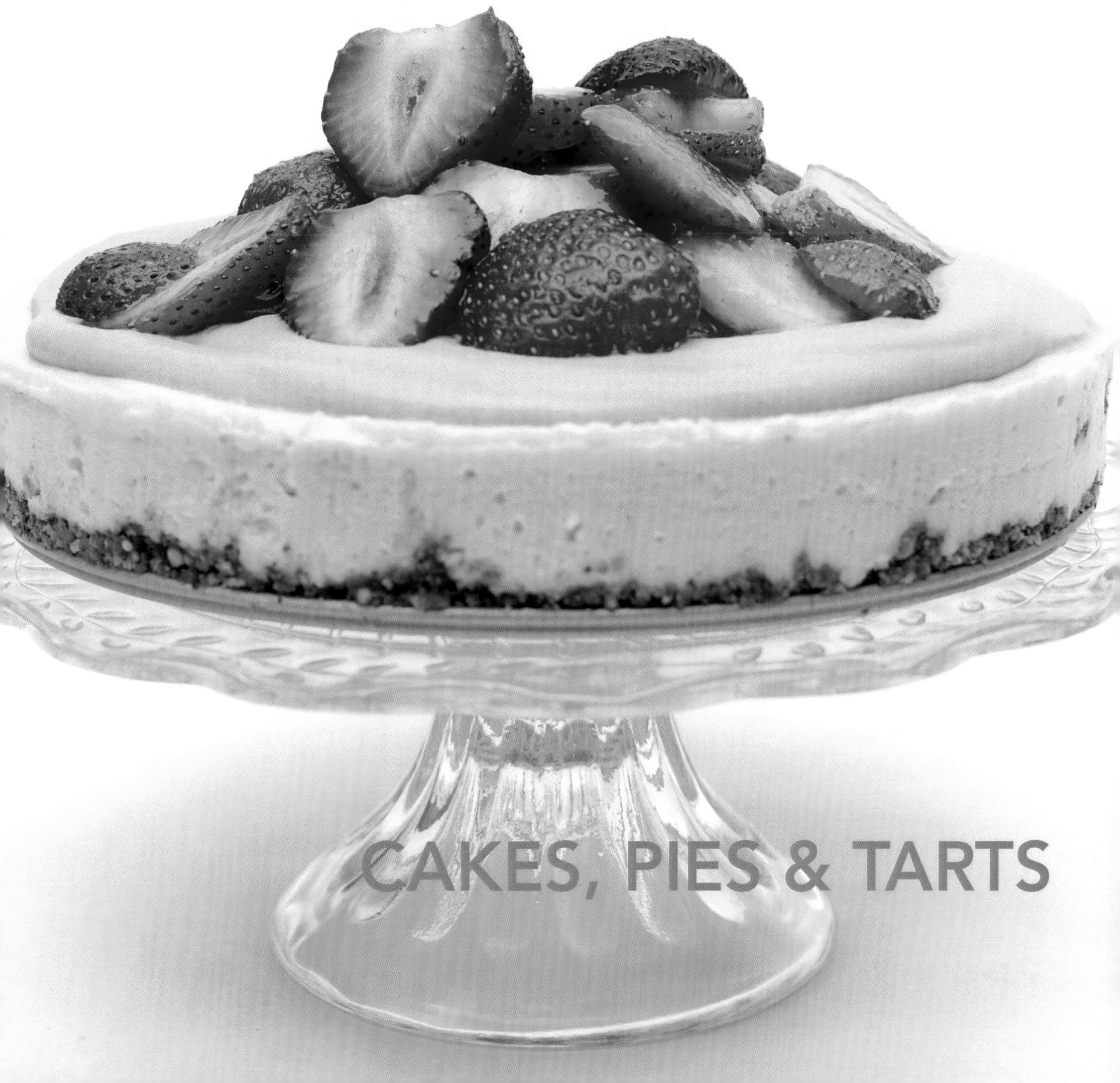

CAKES, PIES & TARTS

CUTIE CUP CAKES

There is something about little, miniature bite-sized desserts that are just so cute – I love 'em!

TIP

For green color icing add a few drops of liquid chlorophyll

For pink add a bit of cranberry powder!

½ cup almonds

½ cup cashews

6-8 medjool dates, pitted & chopped

½ teaspoon vanilla bean powder (or 1 teaspoon vanilla extract)

¼ cup flax meal

½ cup raisins

Blend the almonds and cashews in a food processor until mixture is crumbly. Add dates, vanilla bean powder and flax meal. Mix well. Add raisins and pulse a few times until the mixture holds its shape when pressed together. Shape into little balls and place into mini size baking cups. Cover generously with icing and sprinkles.

For the topping, try topping these cuties with the "sweet vanilla bean" (page 71) or "lemon zing fluff" (page 72).

CARROT "PULP" CAKE

From the first day I began juicing, I could not bring myself to throw away the pulp! I would run it back through the machine or use it in soups. Now carrot pulp has become the main ingredient in this raw carrot cake!

2 cups carrot pulp
2 cups oat flour
1 cup medjool dates, pitted & chopped
1 cup walnuts, chopped
1 teaspoon cinnamon

½ teaspoon nutmeg
2 teaspoons vanilla
3 tablespoons agave nectar
1 cup raisins
2 cups shredded coconut

In a food processor pulse the dates, walnuts, cinnamon, nutmeg, vanilla and agave nectar. Adjust spices to your liking. Combine the nut mixture with the carrot pulp, oat flour, raisins and coconut (reserving some of the coconut for garnishing). Line a bread loaf pan with saran wrap and press carrot cake mixture into pan, folding over the excess saran wrap to cover top of cake. Place in freezer. By freezing the carrot cake it will be easier to spread the icing.

For the topping: right before serving, top the carrot cake with your choice of the "sweet vanilla bean" (page 71) or "cacao fudge frosting" (page 74); sprinkled with fresh grated carrot!

RED, WHITE & GUILT-FREE

This makes for a perfect "Freedom Day" celebration dessert!

CRUST

2 cups raw almonds

½ -1 cup medjool dates, pitted & chopped

1 teaspoon lemon zest

½ teaspoon vanilla extract

BASIC FILLING

3 cups raw cashews, soak 1 hr

¾ cups lemon juice, freshly squeezed

¾ cups agave nectar

½ cup coconut oil, raw

1 teaspoon vanilla extract

TOPPING

mixed berries

For the crust: mix nuts and dates in a food processor. Use pulse to mix in lemon zest and vanilla extract. Do not over mix or it will turn into nut butter! Lightly coat a spring form pan with coconut oil and press in nut mixture (pressing up the sides a bit). Place in freezer until ready to fill.

For the filling: blend all ingredients in a high-speed blender until smooth. Pour into chilled crust and freeze.

For the topping: pile high with mixed berries right before serving!

TIP

Try replacing your vegetable oils such as corn and soy with coconut oil. Better yet, try using coconut oil on your skin as a moisturizer!

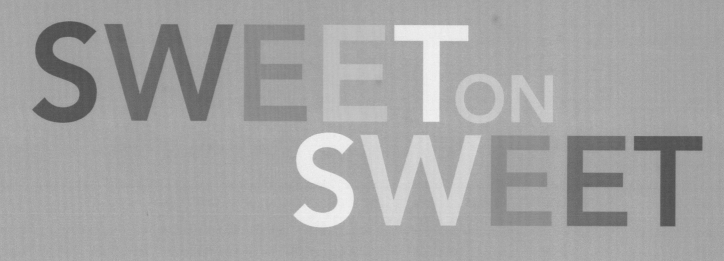

SWEET ON SWEET

I have come to realize that I don't have to have a dessert after every dinner meal! But when I do, I have found some sweet sugar substitutes. We talked a bit about raw honey (page 33), but here are a few more alternatives I keep on hand. Please keep in mind that sugar is not a health food, nor are all the following alternatives natural, so I try to use them sparingly. Most of these substitutes may be bought at a local health food store.

AGAVE NECTAR Is made from the juice of the Agave plant and is said to have a low glycemic level. It is not a natural sweetener, but I still keep a bottle on hand to sweeten my tea and make a few desserts every now and then!

COCONUT PALM SUGAR is derived from the nectar of the coconut palm tree. It has a yummy sweet caramel taste, a low glycemic level and is a perfect alternative to agave syrup or cane sugar.

COCONUT NECTAR Oh yes... this is my favorite! It is a highly nutritious, naturally flowing sap, that flows from coconut blossoms. This sap has a very low glycemic (GI of only 35) level, and has an abundant source of amino acids, B & C vitamins and minerals.

DATE SUGAR is dehydrated dates ground into small pieces. It is a whole food, high in fiber, vitamins, and minerals, and can be substituted for granulated sugar or brown sugar. It is a bit difficult to dissolve but is still one of my favorites!

STEVIA is an herb. Its extracts can have up to 300 times the sweetness of sugar, so you only need a little bit! I prefer the liquid stevia to the powder and usually use a few drops in my home-made kefir drink, mixed with a teaspoon of raw apple cider vinegar.

SUCANAT is unrefined and retains its molasses content. Basically, it's pure dried sugar cane juice and may be used in recipes calling for sugar.

COCONUT MACADAMIA CHEESECAKE

Now all I need is a warm tropical sunset, sand under my feet and the roaring sound of waves in the distance!

TAKE NOTE

Making your own coconut milk is a breeze! Just blend 1 cup young coconut meat with 2 cups water in a high powered blender adjusting the water to your taste!

CRUST

1 cup raw almonds

1 cup raw macadamia nuts

½ -1 cup medjool dates, pitted & chopped

3 teaspoons shredded coconut

½ teaspoon vanilla extract

dash of cinnamon

FILLING

2 cups raw cashews, soaked 1 hour

1 cup raw macadamia nuts, soaked 1 hour

2 cups coconut milk

4 -5 tablespoons lemon juice

¾ cup coconut nectar

¾ cup coconut butter, melted

1 teaspoon vanilla extract

pinch sea salt

TOPPING

fresh shaved coconut

chopped macadamias

drizzle honey date glaze (page 78)

For the crust: finely grind nuts and dates in a food processor. Use pulse to mix in coconut, vanilla and cinnamon. Lightly coat a spring form pan with coconut oil and press in nut mixture (pressing up the sides a bit). Place in freezer until ready to fill.

For the filling: blend all ingredients in a high-speed blender until smooth. Pour into chilled crust and freeze.

For the topping: right before serving, layer on a mixture of fresh shaved coconut and chopped macadamia nuts. Then drizzle generously with my "honey date glaze".

Optional: Agave Nectar may be used in place of the coconut nectar.

STRAWBERRY CLASSIC

There are just some things in life that remain a classic… the strawberry.

CRUST

1 cup raw almonds
½ -1 cup medjool dates, pitted & chopped

¼ cup sucanat
¼ cup coconut oil
pinch of sea salt.

BASIC FILLING

3 cups raw cashews, soaked 1 hr
¾ cup lemon juice
¾ cup agave nectar

¾ cup coconut oil
1 teaspoon vanilla extract

TOPPING

pink cashew frosting (page 74)   fresh strawberries

For the crust: blend the almonds, dates, sucanat and salt in a food processor. Drizzle in coconut oil and pulse to mix. Lightly coat a spring form pan with coconut oil and press in nut mixture (pressing up the sides a bit). Place in freezer until ready to fill.

For the filling: blend all ingredients in a high-speed blender until smooth. Pour into chilled crust and freeze.

For the topping: right before serving, frost with "pink cashew frosting" and then layer with strawberries.

PEACH CRISP

When you grow up in a family of outstanding cooks, one dessert that a meal was not to be without was a peach, apple or cherry crisp…. so to keep tradition in the family, I put a new twist on the crisp!

FILLING

6-8 fresh peaches, sliced thin
2 teaspoons cinnamon
¼ cup raw sugar
½ teaspoon nutmeg, freshly grated

1 teaspoon vanilla extract
1 peach, chopped
¼ cup maple syrup

CRISP TOPPING

2 cups raw walnuts
½ cup medjool dates, pitted & chopped
1 teaspoon coconut palm sugar

1 teaspoon cinnamon
½ teaspoon vanilla powder
pinch of sea salt

TIP

If you choose to eat a bit differently from the way you were raised, it's important to remember… life is not all about food, it's about relationships.

For the filling: it will depend on how big and how deep of a crisp you want. So as all great cooks, just taste as you go! Once sliced, coat the peaches with the cinnamon, sugar, freshly grated nutmeg and vanilla. Then layer in the deep dish pan of your choice.

Next, take 1 peach and blend in a high-powered blender with maple syrup (not raw) to taste. Pour over sliced peaches just enough to make a little bit of juice. If you are using fresh peaches that have been frozen, you will not need to make this peach juice as the frozen ones will already have enough juice in them.

For the crisp topping: blend all ingredients in a food processor to a "crumble", adjusting the spices to your taste. Crumble over the sliced peach mixture and warm in a dehydrator on 105° for 30 minutes before serving. Try paring it with a scoop of "simply vanilla" ice cream (page 83), dusted with cinnamon!

FAMILY
GATHERINGS

My family is big on tradition, especially when it comes to the holidays. Being a vegetarian and maintaining a diet of about 70% raw food, I have discovered a few tips when attending family gatherings. This helps me maintain peace in my heart and unity in the home!

DESSERT. I don't know of anyone who doesn't love desserts! Desserts are a great way to introduce raw food – even for those who are not interested! Besides, who says you have to say it's raw?

GREENS. Try taking a fancy colorful veggie tray to your next family gathering. Or add cranberries and walnuts to a spinach and kale salad for a festive look. That always puts a smile on everyone's face!

LEAVE THE "LOOK" HOME. You know the "look". The one that speaks a thousand words without even saying one. The one that makes a judgment with just one lift of the brow and communicates "Ewww… you are going to eat that?" But rather focus on fun, family and leave that "look" at home.

GIVE THE GIFT OF GRACE. What your family or friends eat is actually none of your business. You are responsible for you and you only. Come to think of it – that in itself is freeing. That is grace.

BE THANKFUL. Perhaps the most important reminder at family gatherings is to relax and enjoy. Pause for a moment and make a mental list of all the things for which you are thankful. For me, I'm thankful for God's provision in my life, my health, and most of all my family.

FROZEN NUT BUTTER TOFU PIE

Living in Southeast Asia for fifteen years, I learned to create all kinds of recipes with tofu!

CRUST

1 cup raw almonds

½-1 cup medjool dates, pitted & chopped

¼ cup carob powder

½ cup shredded coconut

FILLING

1 block of firm tofu

¾ cup almond butter

¾ cup sesame butter

½ cup agave nectar

1 teaspoon vanilla extract

½ teaspoon almond extract

TOPPING

cinnamon almond crème (page 71)   liquid chocolate (page 79)

For the crust: blend the almonds, dates, carob powder and coconut in a food processor. Lightly coat a spring form pan with coconut oil and press in nut mixture (pressing up the sides a bit). Place in freezer until ready to fill.

For the filling: blend the tofu, almond butter, sesame butter, agave nectar, vanilla and almond extract in a high-powered blender until smooth. Adjust sweetness to taste. Pour into chilled crust and freeze.

For the topping: right before serving, slice and top each piece with a dab of cinnamon almond crème drizzled with liquid chocolate.

TANGY CITRUS PIE

My second greatest joy is seeing eyes light up when they take their first bite. My first greatest joy is telling them what's in it!

CRUST

1 cup raw macadamia	½ cup shredded coconut
½ cup pistachio nuts	3-4 dried apricots, diced
½-1 cup medjool dates, pitted & chopped	1 tablespoon lemon zest

FILLING

3 avocados	1 teaspoon vanilla extract
¾ cup fresh lime juice	¼ cup coconut milk
⅓ cup agave nectar	½ cup coconut oil

TOPPING

sweet vanilla bean (page 71)	liquid chocolate (page 79)

For the crust: blend the macadamias, pistachio and dates in a food processor. Next toss in the coconut, apricots and lemon zest and pulse a few times. Love the color! Lightly coat a spring form pan with coconut oil and press in nut mixture (pressing up the sides a bit). Place in freezer until ready to fill.

For the filling: blend avocados, lime juice, agave nectar, vanilla, coconut milk and coconut oil in a high-powered blender until smooth. Adjust sweetener to your taste. Pour into chilled crust and freeze. You are then ready to dish it up!

For the topping: slice and top each piece with a dollop of "sweet vanilla bean" and drizzled with "liquid chocolate".

TIP

Apricots are an excellent source of beta-carotene promoting healthy eyesight and are also a great way to add more fiber to your diet!

BERRY ENOUGH CHEESECAKES

When it comes to desserts our family always says, "give me just a sliver". Next thing you know you have eaten so many "slivers" that you almost down a whole pie! So these little "berry enough" cheesecakes are perfect size for "just a sliver".

CRUST

1½ cup walnuts

½ cup medjool dates, pitted & chopped

½ cup currants

¼ cup date sugar

1 cup shredded coconut

BASIC FILLING

3 cups raw cashews, soaked 1 hr

¾ cup lemon juice

¾ cup agave nectar

¾ cup coconut oil

1 teaspoon vanilla extract

For the crust: blend the walnuts, dates, currants and date sugar in a food processor. Add coconut and pulse a few more times. Lightly coat individual mini cheesecake molds with coconut oil and press approximately 1 tablespoon of nut mixture into each mold. Place in freezer until ready to fill.

For the filling: blend all ingredients in high-speed blender until smooth. Fill the individual molds and freeze.

For the topping: frost with strawberry, blackberry or raspberry glaze (page 75). Then add assorted berries for the final touches!

MORE THAN JUST
FOOD
DID YOU KNOW?

Many of the ingredients I use in my "Sweet Encounter" raw dessert recipes are taken directly from Song of Solomon in the Bible. Dates, nuts, seeds, spices, grapes, raisins, honey, figs, pomegranates, apples and apricots are just a few of the ingredients you will find throughout all of my mouth watering raw dessert recipes (with the exception of a few not being raw)!

Did you know...

Song of Solomon is a Jewish love song between a man and woman. It is meant to appeal to all of our senses. This love song is not just to be sung, but is to be experienced! It's meant to speak to our hearts and not our minds. Song of Solomon resonates within our whole being; spirit, soul, and body, which long for more than just food. We long for love - to be loved and to love.

So more than just food, reading Song of Solomon will tap into all of our hearts and stir emotions we didn't even know we had! But what is really exciting to me, is when we come to know and experience the author behind this Song of all Songs. Not only will healing and restoration take place in our lives, but our approach on the topics of marriage, love, sexual intimacy and food will be looked at much differently!

PECAN SQUARES

You know the little pecan pies you can purchase at a truck stop? Well here's my version!

CRUST

1 cup raw macadamias
½ cup shredded coconut
pinch of sea salt

1 tablespoon of coconut oil
2 teaspoons coconut nectar

FILLING

½ cup cashew butter
½ cup honey date paste (page 78)
3 tablespoons coconut oil
2 tablespoons maple syrup, (grade B)
1 teaspoon cinnamon

1 teaspoon vanilla extract
1 – 3 tablespoons fresh orange juice
3 cups raw pecans, pieces (reserving 1 cup for topping)

For the crust: blend the macadamias in a food processor until very fine. Add coconut and sea salt and blend. Drizzle in coconut oil and coconut nectar, pulsing a few more times to evenly mix. Lightly coat mini "lift and serve" square molds with coconut oil and press approximately 1 tablespoon of nut mixture into each mold. Place in freezer until ready to fill.

For the filling: blend all ingredients (except pecan pieces) in a high-speed blender until smooth, adding just enough orange juice to make a thick creamy paste. Pour mixture into a glass bowl and fold in the pecan pieces. With a tablespoon, place the date mixture into individual molds, smoothing evenly. Sprinkle with more pecans and press gently into the filling. Place in freezer until ready to serve!

Nut Butter: Blend nuts of your choice in a food processor until very fine. Continue blending and after a few minutes the nuts create their own oil and the mixture will turn into the consistency of dough. You might have to add a few drops of water to help it along! Continue blending and it will then go from dough to a batter texture. Add a pinch of salt and some agave nectar to sweeten it up!

FIG-TASTIC TART

I never thought about creating something with figs until I read Song of Solomon. Figs and Song of Solomon had one thing in common. They both were intimidating to me - but not anymore!

CRUST

1½ cup walnuts
½ cup brazil nuts
1 cup medjool dates, pitted & chopped
¼ cup cacao powder
¼ cup of raisins
¼ cup grated coconut
¼ cup sweet cacao nibs

For the crust: blend the walnuts, brazil nuts, dates and cacao powder in a food processor until it holds together. Remember not "over" blend or it will turn into nut butter! Then add the raisins, coconut and cacao nibs, pulsing just enough to mix them in without totally disappearing! Lightly coat a spring form tart pan with coconut oil and press in nut mixture (pressing up the sides a bit).

Place in freezer until ready to fill.

CACAO CARAMEL SAUCE

½ cup coconut oil, melted
¼ cup of maple syrup, (grade B)
½ cup honey date paste (page 78)
¼ cup cacao powder
½ teaspoon cinnamon
½ vanilla bean, scraped
½ teaspoon mesquite powder (optional)

For the sauce: blend all ingredients in a high-powered blender until creamy. Spread an even layer over the chilled crust. Chill once more.

FILLING

3 cups raw cashews, soaked 1 hour

¾ cups lemon juice
¾ cup coconut nectar
½ cup coconut oil
1 vanilla bean, scraped

For the filling: blend ingredients in a high-powered blender until creamy and pour over top of the sauce.

TOPPING

Fresh sliced figs drizzled with coconut nectar and dusted with cinnamon

For the topping: slice fresh figs and gently press them into the filling in a layered fashion, or dare to read "Song of Solomon" and choose another fruit of your choice!

Drizzle coconut nectar over the figs and dust with cinnamon.

PUDDINGS, DIPS & TOPPINGS

PUDDINGS, DIPS & TOPPINGS

emerald dream pudding

say cheesecake pudding

chocolate forest pudding

coconut chip pudding

butterscotch malt pudding

cacao almond pudding

avo-applesauce

chocolate & red raspberry parfait

**SUGGESTED READING FOR
RAW FOOD EATING**

sweet vanilla bean

cinnamon almond crème

lemon zing fluff

cacao caramel sauce

milk chocolate dip

apple date dip

pink cashew frosting

cacao fudge frosting

ginger lemon frosting

berry glaze

SUPERFOODS — 4 of my Favorites

poppy seed glaze

honey date paste

liquid chocolate

EMERALD DREAM PUDDING

The biggest and cheapest avocados are without a doubt found in Indonesia!

2-3 ripe avocados
2-3 limes, persian

⅓ cup agave nectar
1 teaspoon vanilla extract

Blend avocados, limes, agave and vanilla in a high-powered blender until really creamy. Adjust sweet-n-sour tastes to your liking.

Optional:

• Try adding a layer of chocolate forest pudding (page 66), topped with a spoon full of sweet vanilla bean (page 71) and sprinkled with raw cacao nibs!

• To use the pudding as a pie filling add 2 tablespoons of coconut oil to make it a bit thicker when chilled!

TIP

If you ever get a chance to visit Indonesia, make sure you order their avocado drink! First they drizzle the chocolate all around the inside of the glass and then pour in the blended avocado... so creative!

SAY CHEESECAKE PUDDING

Ok… so this is not a so-called traditional "cheesecake" that is laden with pounds of cream cheese, but it sure does make for a great alternative!

1 cup young coconut meat
¼ cup lemon juice, fresh
⅓ cup raw honey

2 tablespoons maple syrup (grade B)
½ vanilla bean, scraped

Blend coconut meat, lemon juice, honey, maple syrup and vanilla in a high-powered blender. Adjust tastes to your liking!

CHOCOLATE FOREST PUDDING

This pudding layered with the emerald dream and topped with sweet vanilla bean makes the ultimate pudding parfait!

2 cups raw cashews, soaked 1 hr
1 cup almond milk
¼ cup agave nectar
1 cup carob powder

½ cup coconut butter
1 vanilla bean, scraped
dash of cinnamon, freshly grated

Blend cashews, almond milk, agave, carob powder, coconut butter and vanilla bean in a high-powered blender until thick and creamy. Pour into a fancy glass; grate some cinnamon over the top and chill until ready to serve.

Optional: to assemble the layered version of this pudding parfait, begin with a layer of chocolate forest pudding, a layer of the emerald dream pudding (page 65), top with a dab of sweet vanilla bean (page 71) and dust with cacao shavings!

COCONUT CHIP PUDDING

This took me about 15 min to make… crackin' the coconut and all!

1 cup young coconut meat
½ cup coconut water
1 tablespoon coconut butter

2 tablespoons agave nectar
½ teaspoon vanilla bean powder

Blend coconut meat, coconut water, coconut butter, agave and vanilla bean powder in a high-powered blender until creamy smooth. Pour into cute little glasses, pile high with coconut chips, chill until ready to serve.

TIP

In Mexico, cinnamon is used in chocolate. In the Middle East it is used to savor dishes such as lamb and chicken and in Persian cuisine, cinnamon is used in soups, desserts and drinks. As a little girl growing up in America, we mixed it with sugar, sprinkled it on toast and then broiled it for a few seconds until it bubbled!

BUTTERSCOTCH MALT PUDDING

Butterscotch and I go way back. Let me introduce it once again, but this time with a malty taste.

1 cup raw cashews, soaked 1 hr
¼ cup coconut oil
1 teaspoon butterscotch extract
2 tablespoons barley malt
1 tablespoon granular soy lecithin
½ teaspoon maca (optional)
almond milk if needed

Blend cashews, coconut oil, butterscotch and barley malt in a high-powered blender until thick and creamy. Add the lecithin and maca with a bit of almond milk if needed to achieve desired thickness. This will thicken as chilled.

TIP

Soy lecithin granules act as an emulsifier and thickening agent. These nutty flavored granules also play a vital role in brain and liver function!

CACAO ALMOND PUDDING

When I'm craving something chocolat-ee, I remind myself of this healthy version!

1½ cup raw almonds
½ cup pure water
½ cup maple syrup (grade B)
½ cup cacao powder
1 teaspoon vanilla extract

Blend almonds in a high-powered blender until powder. Add just enough pure water to make a thick paste. Blend in the maple syrup, cacao and vanilla, process until smooth. Add more pure water if needed. Continue blending until rich, thick and creamy!

AVO-APPLESAUCE

Avocado and apple…. who would have thought? Another one of Johnna's creations in between editing photos!

2 green apples
1 ripe avocado

2 tablespoons agave nectar
fresh lime juice to taste

TIP

The peels from the halved avocado make for great little "bowls" to serve your guacamole in!

Blend apples, avocado and agave in a high-powered blender adding just enough lime juice to make you pucker! Top with sliced apples and serve with a smile.

CHOCOLATE & RED RASPBERRY PARFAIT

There is chocolate and then there is chocolate. This chocolate & red raspberry parfait makes for the perfect date night dessert!

TIP

Parfait is a French word literally meaning "perfect" and began in 1894.

CRUST

1 cup raw almonds
½-1 cup medjool dates, pitted & chopped
¼ cup cacao powder
½ cup sweet cacao chips

FILLING

2 cups almond butter
½ cup maple syrup (grade B)
2-3 tblsp coconut palm sugar
½ cup cacao powder
pinch of sea salt
¼ cup coconut oil
1 teaspoon vanilla extract
¼ cup of red raspberry juice*

TOPPING

fresh red raspberries

For the crust: blend the almonds, dates, cacao powder and cacao chips in a food processor until crumbly. Proceed to press approximately 2-3 tablespoons of the nut mixture gently into individual parfait glasses. Chill in refrigerator until ready to fill.

For the filling: blend almond butter, maple syrup, palm sugar, cacao, sea salt, coconut oil, vanilla and raspberry juice until smooth. Add a little pure water if needed and adjust sweetness to your taste. Continue blending until creamy. Pour into individual parfait glasses and chill once again in refrigerator. Top with red raspberries right before serving. Enjoy your date night!

*Red raspberry juice: The liquid from thawed organic red raspberries makes a great juice!

Optional: try adding a layer of "sweet vanilla bean" crème (page 71) in between the crust and chocolate pudding!

A photo is featured on page 62.

SUGGESTED
READING FOR
RAW FOOD EATING

Here are some of my favorite authors that gave me a great start with learning what raw food eating was all about. I highly recommend beginning with "The Complete Book of Raw Food" by Lori Baird and Julie Rodwell, as it has over 350 recipes from amazing Raw Food Chefs from all over the world. What a great way to graze from a variety of authors and choose which recipes fit you and your lifestyle! This list is far from being exhaustive but will definitely give you a great start as it did me.

Ani's Raw Food Kitchen: *Ani Phyo*

Green for Life: *Victoria Boutenko*

Juicing for Life: *Cherie Calbom & Maureen Keane*

Living Cuisine, The Art and Spirit of Raw Foods: *Renee Loux Underkoffler*

Raw: *Charlie Trotter & Roxanne Klein*

Raw Food – Real World: *Matthew Kenney & Sarma Melngailis*

Raw: The Uncook Book: *Juliano Brotman*

Rawvolution: *Matt Amsden*

The Complete Book of Raw Food: *Lori Baird & Julie Rodwell*

The Live Food Factor: *Susan Schenck*

The Raw Food Detox Book: *Natalia Rose*

The Raw Gourmet: *Nomi Shannon*

SWEET VANILLA BEAN

Basic but elegant, this crème can stand alone, served as a fruit dip, pie topping, or layered with another pudding and served as a parfait. You choose!

1½ cups raw cashews, soaked, 1 hour
½ cup fresh orange juice
2 medjool dates, seeded

1 tablespoon agave nectar
1 vanilla bean, scraped
1 tablespoon coconut oil

Blend cashews, orange juice, dates, agave and vanilla bean in a high-powered blender, until a thick creamy consistency (adding more liquid if necessary). Drizzle in the coconut oil and continue to blend. Chill and serve.

TIP

Raw almonds are known as the "King of Nuts!" They are high in protein, easily digested when soaked, and improves regulation of blood sugar.

CINNAMON ALMOND CRÈME

Fresh grated cinnamon stick is always the best tasting but if you don't have a cinnamon stick around… ground will do.

1½ cups raw almonds, soaked overnight, skins removed
¼ cup lemon juice, fresh
2 tablespoons date sugar

1 teaspoon almond extract
1 teaspoon vanilla extract
½ teaspoon cinnamon
1 tablespoon coconut oil

Blend almonds, lemon juice, sugar, almond extract, vanilla extract and cinnamon in a high-powered blender until smooth, adding more liquid if necessary. Drizzle in the coconut oil and continue to blend. Chill and serve.

LEMON ZING FLUFF

Oh my... topping it with "sweet vanilla bean" (page 71) is all that is needed to complete this masterpiece!

1 cup raw cashews, soaked for 1 hour

½ cup lemon juice, fresh

¼ cup agave nectar

1 teaspoon vanilla extract

¼ cup coconut oil

1 teaspoon lemon zest

Blend cashews, lemon, agave and vanilla until smooth. Drizzle in the coconut oil, add lemon zest and continue to blend. Chill and serve, that is if you can wait that long!

CACAO CARAMEL SAUCE

This is what makes the Fig Tart taste so Fig-tastic! (page 61)

½ cup coconut oil, melted

¼ cup of maple syrup, (grade B)

½ cup honey date paste (page 78)

¼ cup cacao powder

½ teaspoon cinnamon

½ vanilla bean, scraped

½ teaspoon mesquite powder (optional)

Set the jar of coconut oil in a pan of warm water until the amount needed is melted. Or, warm it in a dehydrator on 105° for approximately 20 minutes. Blend all ingredients in a high-powered blender until silky smooth. Chill in refrigerator to thicken. For a thicker sauce add more coconut oil, for thinner add less.

MILK CHOCOLATE DIP

Worth every penny...

1 cup raw almonds, soaked overnight
¼-½ cup pure water
¼-½ cup maple syrup (grade B)

1 teaspoon of vanilla extract
¼ to ½ cup cacao powder
½ teaspoon lucuma powder (optional)

Blend almonds in high-powered blender until very fine. Add maple syrup and vanilla and blend well, adding just enough of the fresh water to make a thick sauce. Slowly add the cacao powder and lucuma powder to taste. For a thicker dip add more almonds, but for thinner, add more water.

Optional: Carob powder may be used in place of cacao.

Note: All chocolate comes from the Cacao Bean. These beans were so revered by the Aztecs and Mayans that they used them as money! (Wished that was still true for today!)

APPLE DATE DIP

This is one time you can double dip your sliced apples and oranges!

3 red apples
1 cup medjool dates, pitted

1 teaspoon mesquite powder (optional)
½ vanilla bean, scraped

Blend apples, dates, mesquite powder and vanilla in a high-powered blender until very creamy. If you want a thicker dip, add more dates and dip until your heart's content!

PINK CASHEW FROSTING

This yummy frosting is a perfect topping for any dessert!

½ cup raw cashews, soaked 1 hr
2 cups frozen strawberries
¼ cup agave nectar

1 teaspoon vanilla extract
¼ cup coconut oil

Blend cashews, strawberries, agave and vanilla until smooth. Drizzle in the coconut oil and continue to blend. Chill until ready to parTAY!

CACAO FUDGE FROSTING

As a little girl I always got to lick the spoon… as a big girl I haven't stopped.

¼ cup coconut butter
½ cup dark agave nectar
½ cup cacao powder

½ teaspoon vanilla extract
Pinch of sea salt

Blend the coconut butter, agave, cacao, vanilla and sea salt in high-powered blender until glossy smooth and then go ahead – lick the spoon!

Optional: Carob powder may be used in place of cacao.

TIP

Don't let this little berry fool ya! The strawberry has a unique combination of antioxidant and anti-inflammatory nutrients, and has been cultivated since the 16th century!

GINGER LEMON FROSTING

The smooth taste of a meyer lemon fused with the bold taste of fresh ginger will leave you craving for more!

1 cup raw cashews, soaked for 1 hour
½ inch piece of ginger

½ cup fresh meyer lemon juice
¼ cup agave nectar
1 vanilla bean, scraped

Blend cashews, ginger, lemon juice, agave nectar, and vanilla bean in high-powered blender until creamy. If you desire a thinner frosting, add more lemon juice with a tad bit of pure water. After applying the frosting to the dessert of your choice, top with freshly grated lemon zest!

BERRY GLAZE

This takes no time to make and is a perfect match for those little "berry enough cheesecakes"!

3 cups frozen berries
agave nectar to taste

1 tablespoon coconut oil

Place frozen berries in a glass bowl and thaw at room temperature. Once they begin to thaw, strain the fruit through a fine mesh nylon strainer while applying pressure to the fruit with the back of a wooden spoon. This will strain out those small tiny seeds. (A metal strainer may also be used but I prefer the nylon. Not for sure why, I just do!)

Pour the fruit liquid into a high-powered blender, adding agave and coconut oil mixing well. The coconut oil will slightly thicken the glaze when chilled.

Optional: Any type of frozen berries may be used. Strawberry, blackberry and raspberry are three of my favorites.

A photo using berry glaze is featured on page 56.

TIP

One of my favorite kitchen gadgets (I have many!) is my "microplane" zester & grater. It does wonders with grating fresh ginger.

SUPERFOODS — 4 FAVORITES!

Superfoods are a great source of antioxidants, essential nutrients, jam-packed with health benefits, and if that is not enough - they are low in calories too! On the other hand, there is not a legal definition of the actual term "superfoods" nor is it a common word among some circles, as they seem to argue about any health benefits in them at all. Superfoods or not, you decide. Here are four of my favorites!

LUCUMA POWDER

Native to Peru, Ecuador & Chile, Lucuma is highly revered as the "Gold of the Incas". With a bold maple-like flavor, this dried exotic fruit is very similar in texture to a hard-boiled egg yolk hence the name "egg fruit". One tree can produce as many as five hundred fruits during a year!

- Nutty maple flavor
- Low glycemic and low in acid
- High levels of beta-carotene, iron, B1, B2 & B3
- Great alternative for agave nectar
- Blends well in smoothies, puddings & ice creams
- May be used as flour in any cooked or raw dish, especially desserts!
- Rich in carbohydrates, fiber, niacin, iron, calcium and phosphorus

MACA POWDER

This power-house Peruvian food is known to increase energy, endurance, physical strength, and libido! It is said that the ancient Incan warriors would devour this potent root before going into battle to make them ferociously strong!

- A robust blend of coffee, malted butterscotch & chocolate-ee taste!
- Boost immune system
- Supports fertility
- Balances hormones
- Enhances the endocrine system
- May decrease anxiety
- Improves sexual desire
- Rich in carbohydrates
- High in calcium, vitamin C, fiber, proteins, B1 & B 12

Delicious blended into smoothies, desserts, oatmeal and more. Be adventurous!

MESQUITE POWDER

Mesquite is a leguminous plant grown in regions of South America. The bean pods of this hearty plant are ground into a delicate flour or meal adding a sweet nutty taste to desserts, breads, cookies and can even be tossed in salads. The sugar in Mesquite is in the form of fructose and does not require insulin for metabolism, therefore maintains a constant blood sugar level for long periods of time making it a perfect sweetener for diabetics! Mesquite blends well with any nut based milk and is an excellent addition to any smoothie!

- Sweet molasses-like flavor with a hint of caramel
- Low glycemic
- Excellent form of fiber
- Improves digestion
- High in protein
- Rich in lysine, calcium, magnesium, potassium, iron, zinc, and fiber.

YACON POWDER

A root vegetable harvested in Peru, the Yacon has the texture and flavor very similar to jicama, but slightly sweeter, and is related to the sunflower and Jerusalem artichoke. This perennial plant is also known as the Mexican potato or earth apple. Benefits?

I knew you were going to ask that!

- Sweet molasses flavor
- Low glycemic
- Good digestive aid
- Boost immune system
- Helps balance hormones

Contains sugar known as FOS (fructooligosaccharide), which is undigested therefore good for diabetics.

Available in different forms including tea: drizzle syrup over fresh fruit, add slices to muffins or sweet breads or use the powder as a substitute for white sugar.

POPPY SEED GLAZE

Goodbye powdered sugar. Hello coconut butter.

½ cup coconut butter
½ cup orange juice
2 tablespoons agave

1 teaspoon vanilla extract
½ teaspoon almond extract
1 teaspoon poppy seeds

Blend coconut butter, orange juice, agave, vanilla and almond extract in a high-powered blender until smooth and creamy! Pour into separate bowl and stir in the poppy seeds. For a thinner glaze add more orange juice, for thicker add more coconut butter.

HONEY DATE PASTE

At first I thought making date paste and nut butters were way out of my league. But now with my food processor and high-powered blender, I not only stay in the game, but hit a home run every time!

1 cup medjool dates, pitted, chopped

2-3 tablespoons raw honey
1 teaspoon vanilla extract

Blend date paste, honey and vanilla in a food processor until smooth.

Optional: to make "**honey date glaze**" add a little bit of orange juice or apple juice to desired consistency.

LIQUID CHOCOLATE

Keeping this syrup refrigerated in a plastic squirt bottle helps me to be ready, aim and squeeze at any time!

1 cup maple syrup
1 cup cacao powder
1 teaspoon vanilla extract

1 teaspoon coconut oil
pinch of sea salt

Blend maple syrup, cacao powder (amount depends on the taste, thickness and the shade of chocolate you want), vanilla, coconut oil and salt in a high-powered blender. This will thicken as chilled so make sure you set it out to soften a bit before "squeezing"!

TIP

Remove the seeds from the dates, fill the cavity with almond butter and top with fresh grated coconut!

ICE CREAMS & MORE

ICE CREAMS & MORE!

simply vanilla ice cream

lemon thyme ice cream

mint chip parfait

purple passion ice cream

hazelnut berry ice cream

apple cinnamon nut crunch

Mom's apple pie ice cream

pomegranate ice cream

raw banana split

A TOAST TO SOLOMON

winter compote

fun-due for two

saucy apple

coconut ice cubes

raw mint brownie sundae

POPSICLES

blueberry & maca pops

blackberry & kale pops

orange crème pops

SIMPLY VANILLA ICE CREAM

In Malaysia, ice cream is spelled – "ais krim". My family and I learned very quickly; culture is not wrong, it's just different!

3 cups almond milk, strained
2 cups raw cashews, soaked 1 hr
2-3 tablespoons agave nectar

½ vanilla bean, scraped
1 cup frozen bananas (optional)

Blend almond milk, cashews, agave nectar and vanilla bean in a high-powered blender until super creamy. Add frozen bananas to desired thickness. Pour into an ice cream maker and process according to the manufacturer's instructions. Scoop–n-serve.

LEMON THYME ICE CREAM

Minced thyme in ice cream is actually quite refreshing!

3 cups almond milk, strained
¼ cup agave nectar
⅓ cup fresh lemon juice

1 teaspoon vanilla extract
1 tablespoon lemon thyme, minced
1 teaspoon lemon zest

Blend almond milk, agave nectar, lemon juice, vanilla extract and minced lemon thyme in a high-powered blender until creamy. Stir in the lemon zest, adjusting flavors if needed. Pour into an ice cream maker and process according to the manufacturer's instructions. Garnish with a few sprigs of lemon thyme and julienne lemon strips! Served in Granny's fancy metal ice cream dishes as featured on page 80.

Note: The nut milks used in the following recipes may be found on page 14.

If you are using organic fruits, such as apples or pears, there is no need to peel.

MINT CHIP PARFAIT

In Hong Kong we ordered chocolate chip ice cream. They brought us a bowl of chocolate ice cream surrounded with potato chips. How creative is that! Here's my take on it.

3 cups almond milk, strained

1½ cups raw cashews, soaked 1 hr

3-4 teaspoons fresh mint leaves, chopped

2-3 tablespoons agave nectar

1 teaspoon vanilla

½ teaspoon peppermint extract

1 teaspoon fresh lemon juice

1 teaspoon lucuma

1 teaspoon liquid chlorophyll for green color

1 cup frozen bananas (optional)

TOPPING

carob chips

liquid chocolate (page 79)

Blend almond milk, cashews, mint leaves, agave nectar, vanilla, peppermint extract, lemon juice, lucuma and chlorophyll in a high-powered blender until super creamy. Add frozen bananas, blending to desired thickness. Pour into an ice cream maker and process according to the manufacturer's instructions. Scoop into pretty parfait glasses, garnish with carob chips and squirt on the liquid chocolate!

TIP

For this ice cream to be really creamy it's important to make sure to strain your almond milk before adding other ingredients.

PURPLE PASSION ICE CREAM

Living in Malaysia for 15 years, grapes were hard to come by. But when we did find them, we would splurge!

3 cups almond milk, strained

2 cups raw cashews, soaked 1 hr

1 cup seedless purple grapes

2-3 tablespoons agave nectar

1 teaspoon vanilla extract

1 tablespoon lucuma (optional)

Blend almond milk, cashews, grapes, agave nectar, vanilla and lucuma in a high-powered blender until super creamy. Pour into an ice cream maker and process according to the manufacturer's instructions. Garnish with edible flowers and a mint leaf!

TIP

I am more concerned what is "in" the food I'm eating than I am in counting calories, but did find it quite interesting that there are 2 calories in 1 grape!

HAZELNUT BERRY ICE CREAM

I always tend to lean towards the almond when making nut milk. This time I wanted to venture out and try something different – the hazelnut.

3 cups hazelnut milk, strained
1 cup frozen raspberries
¼ cup maple syrup (grade B)
½ vanilla bean, scraped

1 cup frozen bananas (optional)

TOPPING
chopped hazelnuts

Make fresh hazelnut milk, strain and set aside. Proceed to blend frozen raspberries, maple syrup and vanilla bean in a high-powered blender until smooth. Add frozen bananas and the hazelnut milk to desired thickness. Pour into an ice cream maker and process according to the manufacturer's instructions. Scoop into fancy cups and garnish with chopped hazelnuts. Yum!

TIP

Hazelnut milk is made the exact same way as almond milk but using hazelnuts instead of almonds! See recipe (page 14)

APPLE CINNAMON NUT CRUNCH

This recipe always reminds me of the traditional Bible dish Haroseth, which was served at Passover to symbolize the mortar the Hebrew slaves used to build Pharaoh's pyramids!

3 apples
½ cup dates, chopped
½ cup figs, chopped
½ cup pumpkin seeds

½ cup walnuts, chopped
1 teaspoon cinnamon
1 cup almond milk (page 14)

Mix in a bowl chopped apples, dates, figs, pumpkin seeds and walnuts. Sprinkle with cinnamon and pour on the almond milk!

Optional: grape juice may be used in place of the almond milk

MOM'S APPLE PIE ICE CREAM

Whoever heard of apple pie without ice cream? Here I take the best from both worlds and combine into a healthy delectable guilt-free dessert!

TOPPING

Blend almond milk, apple juice, maple syrup, cinnamon, nutmeg and vanilla bean in a high-powered blender until creamy. Add frozen bananas to desired thickness. Pour into an ice cream maker and process according to the manufacturer's instructions. Serve with a generous portion of the walnut topping!

For the topping: blend the walnuts, raisins, sugar, cinnamon, vanilla and sea salt in a food processor until crumbly.

Optional: blend in a healthy portion of the walnut topping mix into the ice cream right before serving!

TIP

Did you know that an apple tree takes four to five years to produce its first fruit? Makes me not only appreciate the apple but more so the farmer who waits!

POMEGRANATE ICE CREAM

Did you know that the number of seeds in one pomegranate can be anywhere from 200 to1400 seeds – amazing!

3 cups almond milk, strained
2 cups raw cashews, soak 1 hr
½ cup pomegranate seeds

2-3 tablespoons agave nectar
½ vanilla bean, scraped
1 cup frozen bananas (optional)

Blend almond milk, cashews, pomegranate seeds, agave nectar and vanilla bean in a high-powered blender until super creamy. Add frozen bananas to desired thickness. Pour into an ice cream maker and process according to the manufacturer's instructions. Garnish with more pomegranate seeds – love the vibrant color of the pomegranate!

A photo is featured on page 80.

TIP

The pomegranate is low in calories and sodium and high in potassium and vitamin C!

RAW BANANA SPLIT

A dessert book is not a dessert book without the traditional banana split!

1 banana
3 scoops simply vanilla ice cream (page 83)
fresh strawberries, sliced
coconut shavings
sweet cacao nibs

1 cherry

TOPPING
liquid chocolate (page 79)
berry glaze (page 75)
cacao caramel sauce (page 72)

Assemble by placing one banana in a dish, top with 3 big scoops of simply vanilla ice cream, pile on the strawberries, coconut shavings and cacao nibs. Generously squeeze on the toppings and strategically top with a cherry.

A TOAST TO SOLOMON

Strengthen me with raisins; refresh me with apples, for I am faint with love!
Song of Solomon 2:5

2 apples
2 pears
2-3 dates
2-3 apricots
2-3 figs

½ cup walnuts
handfull of goji berries
½ teaspoon allspice
1 cup grape juice

Mix in a bowl chopped apples, pears, dates, apricots and figs. Toss in the coarsely chopped walnuts and a handful of goji berries. Serve in a fancy glass sprinkled with allspice and drenched with grape juice. Definitely enough to serve two!

TIP

Song of Solomon is no ordinary love song. Reading it will awaken all your senses- including your taste buds.

WINTER COMPOTE

In the winter months eating raw can be a challenge. I find that adding nuts and seeds to my bowl of fruit, revs up my body temperature – just a bit!

2 pears
1 banana
¼ cup walnuts
¼ cup almonds

½ cup blueberries
sunflower seeds
almond milk (page 14)

Mix in a bowl chopped pears and sliced bananas. Add the walnuts, almonds, blueberries and a few sunflower seeds. Stir well as you add the almond milk.

A photo is featured on page 2.

TIP

I just discovered that "compote" is a French word for "mixture". Learning something new every day keeps you feeling young!

FUN-DUE FOR TWO

oranges   strawberries
apples   cherries

FOR THE DIPS...

milk chocolate dip (page 73)   **pink cashew frosting (page 74)**

Slice the oranges and apples. Leave the stems on the strawberries and cherries. Plate it in a fancy serving dish and dip away!

Note: for the pink cashew frosting omit the coconut oil so it is a thinner sauce!

TIP

Try figs dipped in chocolate sauce and then dipped again in nuts or grated coconut for another great fun-due idea!

SAUCY APPLE

My son Josh loves applesauce. Instead of serving him the kind with all the additives, I make it fresh!

2–3 apples
1 tablespoon agave nectar

1 teaspoon cinnamon

Blend chopped apples, agave nectar and cinnamon in a food processor until chunky. For a smoother texture you may use a high-powered blender.

COCONUT ICE CUBES

All the comforts of the tropics blended into one little square!

½ cup raw almonds
1½ cups coconut milk
1 cup frozen bananas
1 cup frozen pineapple, diced

¼ cup maple syrup (grade B)
1 teaspoon cinnamon
1 teaspoon vanilla extract
½ cup shredded coconut

Blend almonds and coconut milk in a high-powered blender (straining is optional). Add bananas, pineapple, maple syrup, cinnamon and vanilla until creamy. Stir in shredded coconut, pour into ice cube trays and freeze. Pop one out and add to your favorite glass of juice or better yet, try adding a whole tray of these tropical cubes to your next party punch!

RAW MINT BROWNIE SUNDAE

You are going to flip when you sink your teeth into this raw mint brownie sundae! Let's begin by talking brownie first…

MINT BROWNIE CHUNKS…

2 cups cashews

2 cups walnuts

1 cup cacao powder

1 tsp cinnamon

6-8 mint leaves (optional)

1/2 cup maple syrup (grade B)

¼ cup agave nectar, dark

1/2 cup water

1/2 vanilla bean – scraped

In a food processor blend cashews and walnuts until powdered. Add cacao powder, cinnamon, mint leaves, maple syrup, agave nectar, water (as needed) and vanilla bean blending well. Adjust ingredients to your taste buds!

Place nut mixture into a 9 x 13 pan lined with wax paper and press evenly into pan. Dehydrate for approximately 12 hours. Lift brownies out of pan, remove wax paper and cut into squares. Place each brownie square on a mesh dehydrator sheet and continue to dehydrate for another 6 hours, until crisp on the outside and gooey on the inside.

Set aside a few of the brownies and generously top them with "cacao fudge frosting" (page 74) for an "out-of- this-world" dessert experience! Use the rest of the brownies, if you have any left, to continue making your "raw mint brownie sundae"…

NOW FOR THE RAW ICE CREAM…

simply vanilla ice cream (page 83)

THEN THE TOPPING…

cherry

liquid chocolate (page 79)

cacao chips (optional)

Assemble: fill the bottom of your parfait glass with crumbled mint brownie chunks and liquid chocolate. Next add a generous scoop of simply vanilla ice cream, more liquid chocolate and crumbled brownies. Add another scoop of vanilla ice cream topped with a cherry, more liquid chocolate and sprinkle on the cacao chips. Hard to believe this dessert is all raw!

The following popsicles are great for a summer time treat, especially when you have three of the cutest little models who dare to try! Thank you Lovee, Genesis and Millie!

BLUEBERRY MACA POPS

2 cups almond milk (page 14)
1 cup frozen blueberries

1 cup frozen bananas
1 teaspoon maca powder

Blend all ingredients in a high-powered blender for 30-45 seconds adding more frozen bananas to desired thickness if needed. Pour into popsicle molds and freeze.

BLACKBERRY & KALE POPS

2 cups almond milk (page 14)
1 cup frozen blackberries

1 cup frozen bananas
1 - 2 kale leaves

Blend all ingredients in a high-powered blender for 30-45 seconds adding more frozen bananas to desired thickness if needed. Pour into popsicle molds and freeze.

ORANGE CRÈME POPS

2 cups almond milk (page 14)
2 oranges
1 cup frozen bananas

½ vanilla bean, scraped
1 teaspoon of orange zest

Blend all ingredients except the orange zest, in a high-powered blender for 30-45 seconds, adding more frozen bananas to desired thickness if needed. Add the orange zest and pulse a few times. Pour into popsicle molds and freeze.

KEEPING TRADITION

Granny & Gramps in front of "Have-a-Snack" Café

STANDARD GROCERY

OPALINE

KEEPING TRADITION

KEEPING
TRADITION

My daughter Johnna always reminds me, "Mom, it's not about food it's about relationships". Oh so true. Yes, I'm a vegetarian and yes I eat mostly raw. But when traveling overseas on mission trips or staying stateside and attending family gatherings, I would rather lean more towards the side of grace – choosing relationships rather than being overly concerned with what everyone is eating or not eating.

In keeping with family tradition, I want to crown "Sweet Encounter" with the honors of passing on to you a few of our family's prize winning dessert recipes – loaded with butter, sugar and white flour! I know, I want to cringe at just the thought of those ingredients, but right now it's not about the food, it's about family. Besides, these are the desserts I grew up on and Momma says I turned out ok!

GREAT MOM'S SUGAR COOKIES

This cookie won several blue ribbons at the Missouri State Fair!

1 cup sugar
¾ cup butter
1 teaspoon vanilla
2 eggs

4 cups flour
3 teaspoons baking powder
¼-½ cups milk

TIP

My granny didn't have cookie cutters while growing up, so they would cut shapes out of cardboard, place it on the cookie dough and cut around them with a knife!

Cream sugar and butter. Add vanilla and eggs. Stir in the flour and baking powder, alternating with the milk. Chill and roll out the dough 1/8 inch thick. Cut with floured cookie cutters. Put a raisin in the center and sugar well. More plump if you cook the raisins first.

Bake at 375° until golden brown.

Note: Adding the amount of milk depends on what type of cookie you want. If you want a soft cookie add ½ cup milk and for a crisp cookie add ¼ cup milk.

Great Mom Chamberlain

GRANNY'S GINGERBREAD MEN

As a little girl I loved helping my granny in the kitchen. Standing on a chair to roll out the cookies, the gingerbread man was my all time favorite.

½ cup soft oleo (butter)
½ cup brown sugar
1 egg
½ cup molasses
3 cups flour

½ teaspoon baking soda
½ teaspoon salt
2½ teaspoons ground ginger
½ teaspoon nutmeg

Cream butter and sugar. Add egg and molasses. Stir in the flour, baking soda, salt, ginger and nutmeg. Chill overnight and roll out the dough 1/4 inch thick. Cut with floured ginger bread man cutter. Ice each cookie with "Royal Icing".

Bake at 375° for 5-6 minutes.

ROYAL ICING

2 egg whites
¼ teaspoon cream of tartar
½ teaspoon of vanilla

3 ½ cups powdered sugar
tint as desired with food coloring

Using a hand beater, blend the egg whites, cream of tartar and vanilla in a large bowl.

Gradually add the powdered sugar and continue beating until creamy. Tint with food coloring.

TIP

"Give a little love to a child and you get a great deal back" - Granny Cripe

Granny Cripe teaching Home Economics

COCONUT WASHBOARDS

Remember the old washboard? Here's Granny's cookie to remind you of them!

1 cup of shortening
2 cups brown sugar
2 eggs
4 cups flour

1½ teaspoon baking powder
½ teaspoon baking soda
¼ teaspoon salt
1 cup flaked coconut

Cream shortening, sugar and eggs. Add flour, baking powder, baking soda, salt and continue to blend. Stir in coconut flakes. Roll into about 1 inch long rolls, press the cookie with a fork that has been dipped in sugar.

Bake at 375° until golden brown.

TIP

If we pause to think, we'll have a cause to thank! – Granny Cripe

LILY SALAD

There was no one named Lilly (that I know of!) in our family but this salad was a must at every Christmas gathering. Granny would always crack her own walnuts and pecans so without fail you would find a piece of a shell in a bite or two! Oh yes, she whipped her own cream too!

½ cup milk
4 egg yolks
½ teaspoon mustard
grapes

marshmallows
1 large can pineapple
1 cup nuts
1 pint whip cream

Bring ½ cup milk to a boil. Add 4 egg yolks and ½ teaspoon mustard. Cool and pour over fruit. Let set for 24 hours.

Note: as for the exact amount of each ingredient in this recipe, you will just have to "eye-ball" it as Granny would say. Besides, most of the time no one really measured when it came to cooking in our family!

GRANNY'S CHILDREN RAISING RECIPE

It was always hard to know exactly what was in Granny's recipes as they changed every time. It just depended on what was in her cupboard! But one thing you knew for sure – she loved her children.

1 cup friendly words
2 heaping cups of understanding
4 teaspoons time
4 teaspoons patience

Pinch of warm personality
Dash of humor
a handful of faith in God

Measure words carefully. Add heaping cups of understanding. Use generous amounts of time and patience. Add a dash of humor, a pinch of warm personality and season with the spice of life. Stir in a handful of trust in God. Keep temperature low – do not boil. Serve in individual molds.

DATE ROLL

I was never really fond of mushy dates as a little girl, but always liked to nibble on Granny's date roll.

1 cup cream	dates, chopped
3 cups sugar	2 teaspoons vanilla
¼ teaspoon salt	½ cup nuts

Cook the cream, sugar and salt to soft ball stage. Remove from fire and add chopped dates. Cook till well heated and dates are mushy. Add vanilla and nuts. Beat until stiff.

Prepare a towel dipped in water and rung out. Sprinkle with powdered sugar. Pour candy on towel and make a roll. Slice when cool.

APPLESAUCE CAKE

Sunday dinners were not quite the same without Uncle Kenny, leg propped up on table, salting his chicken and eating his favorite – applesauce cake. I love my uncle Kenny!

½ cup butter	3 ½ cups flour
2 cups white sugar	2 teaspoons cinnamon
1 egg	½ teaspoons cloves
1 teaspoon vanilla	½ teaspoons allspice
2 cups unsweetened applesauce	1 cup nuts
2 teaspoons baking soda	1 cup raisins

Cream butter and sugar. Add egg, vanilla and applesauce (with the soda dissolved in it) and continue to blend with hand mixer. Add dry ingredients and 1 cup nuts, 1 cup raisins and for color you may add midget gum drops!

Bake 350° for 30-35 minutes or until toothpick inserted into the middle of the cake comes out clean.

Johnna, Momma Connie and Kelly

MOM'S TRADITIONAL TWO CRUST PIE

This pie crust has been in our family as long as anyone can remember! Mom has added the vanilla and a little sugar to make a sweet dough.

2 cups flour **1 teaspoon vanilla**
1 cup shortening **2 teaspoons sugar**
add just enough ice water to form a ball.

Pour all ingredients (except water) into a large mixing bowl. Use a fork (and your finger tips) to cut the shortening into the flour. Cut through until the shortening is the size of peas. The key is to keep a light hand and not to over-mix. Slowly add water as needed to form a ball. Divide the dough into two parts. Roll each part out between two pieces of wax paper. Place the first layer in the bottom of the pie pan or baking dish with ½ inch overhang. (Do not stretch the dough.) Fill with your favorite fruit filling and top with the remaining layer. Crimp the top and bottom layer together. Bake between 375°-400° until golden brown. Approximately 45 minutes.

Note: Shortening may consist of all Crisco, all butter or half of each!

TIP

Family secrets for making a flaky pie crust!

1. Use half as much shortening as you do flour. (ex: 2 cups shortening to 4 cups flour)

2. Do not overwork the dough – always keep a light hand!

MOM'S APPLE CRISP

I can still hear my granny's voice "Kelly, the way to a man's heart is through his stomach". This recipe has proven Granny right!

10-12 tart apples (or fruit of your choice)
½ cup brown sugar

2 teaspoons cinnamon
1 teaspoon vanilla

TOPPING

1 cup sugar
1 cup butter

1½ cup flour

For filling: peel and slice apples thin. Place in lightly buttered 13x9 inch pan. Sprinkle with sugar, cinnamon and vanilla. Mix well.

For topping: mix sugar and butter until crumbly then add flour and blend. Spread evenly over filling. Bake at 375°-400° until lightly brown and crisp!

Optional: Blueberries, blackberries, peaches or even rhubarb are some of our families' favorites that are used in place of apples.

TIP

In this health conscious society, my mom declares, "I have given up a lot of things in my lifetime, but still must have my pie in season!" Peach pie in August, apple pie in the fall, cherries in early summer and have your freezer stocked for the winter!

KELLY'S
GADGETS

Some women love flowers; some love chocolate…I love kitchen gadgets. Here are a few of my favorite "must haves"! My number one is more than a gadget, it's the mighty, can't compare to anything, Blendtec® blender! I Use it every day, especially for smoothies. Then there's the first in its league, my 11 cup Cuisinart food processor, great for whipping up raw pie crusts & nut balls. When it comes to a juicer, I settled for nothing less than the Green Star and my dehydrator is ,the one and only 9 shelf Excalibur—all the way. In my kitchen there are Hinckel knives, a special pink handled Kyocera ceramic knife (a gift from my son), lots of mason jars of all sizes, fine mesh strainers, spring form pans, fancy dishes, and glasses of all sorts! Oh, and I can't forget my fermenting jars, mandoline slicer for making uniformed julienne strips, and both the Saladacco and the Spirooli slicers for making zucchini noodles or apple rings! Whew… that was a whirlwind view of my kitchen gadgets!

KELLY'S PANTRY

The following ingredients (not all raw) are typically what you would find at any given moment in my pantry!
This list is not exhaustive, but it will definately give you a well-rounded idea of how I begin to stock up.

DRIED FRUITS
apples
apricots
bananas
blueberries
cherries
coconut
cranberry
dates
figs
goji berries
mango
mulberries
papaya
pineapple
raisins/currants

FRUITS
apples
bananas
blueberries
grapes
kiwi
lemons
limes
oranges
strawberries
young coconut

GRAINS
buckwheat
kamut
millet
oats
quinoa
wheat berries

NUTS
almonds
brazil nuts
cashews
hazelnuts
macadamia
pecans
pine nuts
pistachio
walnuts

NUT BUTTERS
almond
brazil
cashew
hazelnut
macadamia
pecan
sunflower
tahini (sesame seeds)

OILS
coconut butter
coconut oil
fish oil
flax seed oil
safflower oil
virgin olive oil

SEEDS
chia
flax
hemp
poppy
pumpkin
sesame
sunflower

VEGGIES
avocado
beets (red & yellow)
broccoli
cabbage
carrots
cauliflower
celery
cucumber
garlic
greens (dandelion, collards, sorrel, rocket etc)
jicama
kale
onions (spring onions, shallots)
parsley
spinach
tomatoes & sun dried tomato
zucchini

MISCELLANEOUS

SALTY
bragg's liquid amino acid
coconut liquid aminos
miso
nama shoyu
sea salt
seaweed (dulse, kelp, nori, arame, kombu, wakame etc)
tamari

SOUR
apple cider vinegar, raw
coconut vinegar, raw

SPICY
cayenne pepper
chipotle pepper
garlic bulbs
ginger, fresh
jalapeño
wasabi powder

SWEET
agave nectar
bee pollen
blackstrap molasses
cacao powder & sweet nibs
carob powder & chips
coconut nectar, raw
date paste
honey, raw
liquid stevia
maple syrup (grade B)

Plus, I always keep a variety of frozen fruits & bananas for smoothies, dried, and fresh herbs, brewer's yeast, Aloe vera juice, nutritional yeast, spirulina and chlorella powders on hand!

KELLY'S ONLINE SHOPPING

Blendtec® Blender: http://bit.ly/pOSKef

Cultures for Health: http://bit.ly/hx5zpJ

Live Long Eat Raw T-shirts, calendars and more by Johnnabrynn Photography. http://bit.ly/ztSR15

Mountain Rose Herbs: http://bit.ly/hj38ak

Natural Zing: http://bit.ly/bhbCEh

The Raw Food World Store: http://bit.ly/fatcFu

JOHNNA'S BAG

Johnna shoots primarily with ambient, natural lighting using all professional Canon equipment: 5DMarkII body and L-series lenses. Off-camera and on-camera lighting are utilized when necessary. Post processing on 24" Mac desktop and 15" Macbook Pro using Adobe software: Photoshop, Lightroom, InDesign, Bridge and PhotoMechanics. Visit her website to learn more at www.johnnabrynn.com.

JOHNNA'S RAVES

GETS IT

"Johnna gets it… and I don't think that school or years of experiences teaches you "it"… rather, she gets "it" in the observing, anticipating, and being true to her aim with the camera!" -Victoria, Washington DC

GIFTED

"You are gifted, Johnna. Your heart to capture us, just the way we are, telling the story of our lives." -Brenda, Blue Springs MO

AMAZING

"When Johnna took our pictures, she was hidden but there. She captured the most amazing memories in all sorts of formats! Thank you. Johnna!" -Ellen, Myrtle Beach SC

KEEN INSIGHT

"Johnna is amazing, keen insight and full of hope & inspiration." –Adam, Phoenix AZ

APPENDIX

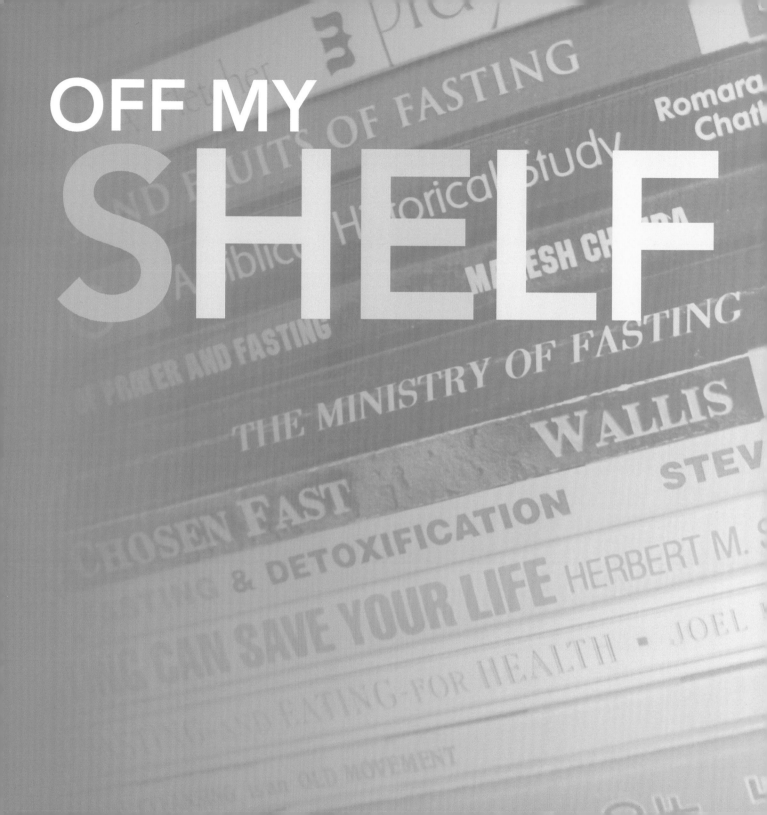

OFF MY

SHELF

When I first realized I needed to make a change in the kitchen, was after stepping off the scale at the doctor's office during one of my annual check-ups. I definitely didn't need another "diet" but needed a complete life change – body, soul and spirit. I knew nothing about juicing, food combining, fasting, let alone eating "raw"! Here are some of the books off my shelf that helped me in the transition to where I am today.

A Hunger for God – John Piper
Mucusless Diet Healing System - Arnold Ehret's
Breaking the Food Seduction – Neal Barnard, M.D.
Dictionary of Natural Foods – William L. Esser
Food Combining for Health – Doris Grant, Jean Joice
Food Combining Made Easy – Herbert Shelton
Food is Your Best Medicine – Henry G. Beiler, M.D.
Juicing for Life – Cherie Calbom, Maureen Keane
Hard to Swallow: The Truth about Food Additives – Doris Sarjeant, Karen Evans
Healing Secrets from the Bible – Dr. Patrick Quillin, PhD, RD, CNS
Mediterranean Diet – Nancy Harmon Jenkins
Prescription for Dietary Wellness - Phyllis A. Balch, CNC, James F. Balch, M.D.
Prescription for Nutritional Healing – Phyllis A. Balch, CNC, James F. Balch, M.D.
Raw Food- Real World -Matthew Kenney & Sarma Melngailis
The Cleanse Cookbook – Christine Dreher
The Complete Book of Raw Food - Lori Baird & Julie Rodwell
The Fit for Life Cookbook – Marilyn Diamond
The Joy of Juicing – Gary Null and Shelly Null
The Liver Cleansing Diet – Sandra Cabot, M.D.
The New Book of Food Combining – Jan Dries
The Raw Food Detox Book -Natalia Rose
The Raw Food Detox Diet – Natalia Rose
The Raw Gourmet -Nomi Shannon
The Vegan Epicure – Hermine Freed
Vegetarian Express – Nava Atlas, Lillian Kayte
Wild Fermentation – Sandor Ellix Katz

INDEX

SMOOTHIES

TRUFFLES & BARS

SIMPLY ENJOY
LIVING

Friend,

May you be healthy in body and strong in spirit. May you be blessed beyond measure and may the generations that follow you prosper abundantly.

Kelly Parr

For all your publishing needs

COOKBOOKS
FICTION
NONFICTION
SELF HELP
INSPIRATIONAL
CHILDRENS

Check us out at http://www.purposepublishing.com/

PURPOSE PUBLISHING

Love this layout?
Meet the designer & see more graphic samples!

VISIT

Sharon Dailey Design

http://www.sharon-designs.com/